PARTICIPATIVE SYSTEMS
AT WORK

PARTICIPATIVE SYSTEMS
AT WORK
Creating Quality
and Employment Security

Edited by
Sidney P. Rubinstein

Introduction by
Senator Bill Bradley

HUMAN SCIENCES PRESS, INC.
72 FIFTH AVENUE
NEW YORK, N.Y. 10011-8004

Printed in the United States of America
987654321

Library of Congess Cataloging-in-Publication Data

Participative systems at work.

Includes index.
1. Management—United States—Employee participation—Congresses. I. Rubinstein, Sidney P.
HD5660.U5P38   1987   658.3'152   86-20044
ISBN 0-89885-338-9

To my parents, Joe and Minnie, garment workers.
Their dreams and values give me
hope and direction.

CONTENTS

7

CONTRIBUTORS

Bill Bradley, US Senator from New Jersey.

Sam Camens, Assistant to the President, United Steelworkers of America, Pittsburgh, Pennsylvania.

John Hoerr, Senior Writer for *Business Week*, New York City.

Clark Leslie, Vice President of Operations at Ethicon, Inc., Sommerville, New Jersey.

Don Pearson, Coordinator/Trainer, Labor-Management Participation Team Process, Interlake, Inc., Riverdale, Illinois; and a Trustee of United Steelworkers of America, Local 1053.

Saul A. Rubinstein, Executive Vice President of Participative Systems, Inc., Princeton, New Jersey; and Consultant to Interlake, Inc., Riverdale, Illinois.

Sidney P. Rubinstein, President of Participative Systems, Inc., Princeton, New Jersey.

Mike Shay, Manager of the Central and South Jersey Joint Board, Amalgamated Clothing & Textile Workers Union, Somerset, New Jersey.

Gerald J. Shope, Manager of Employee Relations at Interlake, Inc., Riverdale, Illinois.

Lynn Williams, International President of the United Steelworkers of America, Pittsburgh, Pennsylvania.

Ralph Yates, Coordinator/Trainer, Labor-Management Participation Team Process, Interlake, Inc., Riverdale, Illinois; and Vice President of the United Steelworkers of America, Local 1053.

ACKNOWLEDGMENTS

I should like to thank my fellow contributors. Their support, creative insights, and encouragement made this book possible. These individuals are among the finest leaders in their fields.

It was professors Ellis R. Ott and Mason Wescott of the Graduate Program in Applied and Mathematical Statistics at Rutgers University who first encouraged me to combine my interest in quality control with issues of relationships and motivation in the workplace.

The first plant where I developed and implemented Participative Quality Control was the Greater New York Box Company, Clifton, New Jersey, in 1959. This was accomplished with the dedicated support of the plant manager and one of the company principals, Jules Edelman.

Irving Bluestone, Wayne State University professor and retired vice president of the United Auto Workers, was responsible for taking the concept of worker participation and making it a national movement. His confidence guided me into the quality of work life field.

I should like to thank Dr. Eizaburo Nishibori, consultant

from the Japanese Standards Association and Dr. Yoshio Kondo from Kyoto University, Japan, for their interest in helping me understand the importance of participative systems in an international context.

A special thanks must go to the workers, supervisors, managers, and union leaders who "stuck with it" in our projects. Among that group are the coordinator/trainers, special people chosen from labor and management who are at the center of activity and serve as a major source of spirit and skills for this process. My associate, Robert Loekle, was in the first group of such coordinator/trainers trained by Professor Ellis Ott and I, for the Amalgamated Lithographers, Local 1, New York, in 1972. To Bob, my associates, the coordinator/trainers, and all the participants; thanks.

I should like also to thank the following people who helped make this book a reality. Editorial assistance and guidance was provided by Robert Strunsky, Raymond E. Disch, and Marc Rubinstein. Preparation of the manuscript through its many drafts and redrafts was provided by Norma Hamilton. And, above all, a very special note of appreciation to my wife, Mae, and family.

Sidney P. Rubinstein

GUIDE TO THE READER

Participative Systems at Work is a collection of viewpoints by individuals who have a deep commitment and interest in the issues of our economy and workplaces. The ideas voiced by these contributors have been shaped over many years by preparations for, and experiences and evaluations of a series of attempts at building new social and technical systems in industry. We have all felt the anticipation, frustration, and satisfaction which accompany these experiences, knowing that this process is, and will continue to be, an evolutionary one. Each stage has grown from an evaluation of prior practices and concepts. We continue to learn, and it is our desire that, by studying this volume, you can find direction for your efforts.

This book was developed from presentations and remarks made at a two-day conference of workers, managers, and union and government officials, which was sponsored by Participative Systems, Inc. in Princeton, New Jersey. The people talk as they normally would, without inhibitions or restraints. The result is a candid, and at times, critical look at the worker participation process.

INTRODUCTION

In the introduction titled, "A Flexible Framework is Needed," Senator Bill Bradley presents an overview of the emerging shape of labor-management relationships in the years ahead. His opening speech set the tone for the conference and provides the introduction for this book.

Bradley provides a vision of the future in which there will be a significant role for labor-management partnerships. A highly competitive economic climate will compel workers and managers jointly to seek improvements in productivity and product quality and, thereby, become more effective as managers of the production process. This will be accomplished through worker representation on boards of directors, labor-management teams on the shop floor, employee ownership, or a combination of some or all of these elements. Furthermore, Bradley believes that one of the keys to the future is a new tax system "to encourage innovation, entrepreneurship and change."

At the same time, a better educated labor force will demand self-fulfillment in the workplace. The convergence of the two trends, the demand for a greater challenge and responsibility in the workplace and the need to be competitive, will bring both long-term economic growth and individual self-fulfillment.

PART I: OVERVIEW

Chapter 1 is an expanded presentation of the keynote address delivered at the conference by Sidney Rubinstein. As president of Participative Systems, Inc., he has been active as a consultant in quality control and labor-management relations for more than 25 years and has taken part in more than 100 projects. Rubinstein cites employment insecurity and archaic organizational structures as the factors which combine to obstruct improvement in quality and productivity in industries throughout the world today. He discusses these problems and suggests solutions based on the Participative Systems model. As illustrations, he reviews two such experiences and the lessons learned from them. He criticizes where criticism is needed, is candid about his

own early projects (some of which were only partially successful), and demonstrates how some experts, particularly those in
quality control, are impeding the development of real participation.

In recent years, Rubinstein has constructed a total plant system of worker participation. This chapter defines the elements
of his plan, which includes a company-wide or plant-wide integration of efforts to build quality products, increase productivity, plan for avoidance of layoffs, and create a team problem-
solving approach that is integrated with labor-management
committees both at departmental and plant-wide levels.

PART II: EXPERIENCE

Interlake Inc.'s Riverdale, Illinois plant has had a successful Labor Management Participation Team program since late
1982. Chapter 2, "The Interlake Experience," was prepared
from a panel presentation by Saul Rubinstein, executive vice
president of Participative Systems, Inc. and three employees of
Interlake Steel: Jerry Shope, manager of employee relations;
Don Pearson, trustee of United Steelworkers Local 1053, and
Ralph Yates, vice president of Local 1053. Pearson and Yates
are also coordinator/trainers in that program, which was based
in large part on concepts developed by Participative Systems,
Inc. This chapter (divided into four sections) tells how the project started, how it was organized, the role strategic planning
plays in the LMPT process, and what the results have been.
With close cooperation between Interlake management and the
USWA Local 1053, the Riverdale plant now has 34 shop floor
teams of workers and supervisors dealing with problem-solving.
It also has middle level advisory committees of union-management representatives and a plant-wide policy committee.

Chapter 3, "The Ethicon Achievement," and chapter 4,
"The Amalgamated Clothing and Textile Workers Union
Achievement," turns to a second example of a worker participation process at Ethicon's Somerville, New Jersey plant. It focuses
on the attitudes, problems, and solutions faced by company and
union leaders in implementing a participative process.

In chapter 3, Clark Leslie, vice president of operations for

Ethicon, Inc., tells of the economic problems that led to a management-union decision to build a new relationship. The company decided that participation would have to be a key ingredient in making the plant competitive. He explains why management decided that it could accept a no-layoff policy as a means of gaining workers' commitment to quality and productivity improvement. Leslie explains the typical problems encountered by management in trying to initiate work reforms. Yet, it is evident in the substance and style of Leslie's presentation that a determined, enlightened management can prevail despite such problems.

In chapter 4, Mike Shay, manager of the Central and South Jersey Joint Board of the Amalgamated Clothing and Textile Workers Union, complements Leslie's presentation by describing problems on the union side in starting and sustaining the Ethicon program. This chapter is an honest account of the many hurdles that must be crossed to implement such a program. Shay stresses that many of the problems originate on the union side and that many workers retain the traditional view that reforms cannot work and that it is useless to try. In the end, however, Shay makes a forceful statement about the necessity of finding new ways of working together.

PART III: PERSPECTIVE

Chapter 5, by Sam Camens, assistant to the president of the United Steelworkers of America, is an impassioned plea for worker participation from one of the labor movement's most effective advocates of the process. A former rank-and-file steelworker and local union president, Camens speaks from more than 40 years of experience in the labor movement. He heads the USWA's effort to establish Labor-Management Participation Teams at the major steel companies.

Camens describes the need to democratize industry, give greater work fulfillment to younger workers and change the steel industry's autocratic method of managing people to a participative method. Camens contends that worker participation amounts to a basic cultural change, one that carries risk for unions but one that unions simply can no longer avoid if they are to remain viable in a new era of competition.

Chapter 6, by Lynn Williams, president of the United Steel-workers of America, is one of the most provocative speeches made recently by a major American labor leader. Williams is a strong advocate of worker participation. Here, he lays out his justification for having unions involved in work reforms.

People want challenging jobs, Williams believes, and he is willing to work with any company that accepts the union and does not try to break it. The central reasoning that Williams applies to union involvement in participation goes like this: the entrepreneurial spirit in America has contributed enormously to the success of the system, particularly in a material way. It has also led to "extreme authoritarianism." A union can tap that spirit by becoming involved with management and, thereby, make the company more competitive (thus saving and creating jobs). At the same time, participation will enable the union to eliminate the old authoritarian structures, give a voice to its members, and provide them with work satisfaction.

Chapter 7, by John Hoerr, senior writer at *Business Week*, reflects his many years as a journalist. It includes his appraisal of the conference, which he attended, and an assessment of the worker participation movement, in general. This chapter does a thorough job of tracing the development of cooperative efforts and closes with Hoerr's personal assessment of some of today's major issues.

Consequently, this book presents concepts and experiences that amount to a virtual revolution in the way work is organized and managed in the United States. It presents direct and vivid evidence on how to put in place the sweeping changes necessary to attain four major goals: improvements in the efficient use of resources; product quality; employment security; and workplace democracy.

INTRODUCTION

A Flexible Framework Is Needed

There is no question that the world is changing and changing rapidly because of technology and automation, international competition, and deregulation. This change brings enormous opportunity as well as some danger. If you look at our economy today you find that 25 percent of our GNP derives from manufacturing. Peter Drucker estimated that by the year 2000 we will continue to receive 25 percent GNP from manufacturing, but instead of that amount being produced with 20 million workers, it will be produced with 5 million.

The prospect of changes in the service industries, which now account for more than 60 percent of our GNP, is just as large. Those changes do not just involve computer technology in our offices, which will make them quite different environments in the years to come; nor are they restricted to changes in traditional industries with computerized design. What I mean is that workers will continue in whatever field, whatever location, to have to deal with an increasingly large amount of information, and this offers a unique opportunity in the area of labor-management relations.

It appears that we have sought individual self-fulfillment in this country in many different ways during the last 15 to 20 years. And what we have come back to is the basic proposition that self-fulfillment will ultimately come from what one does in the workplace. The unique opportunity for our society is that it is precisely a change in the workplace that is essential for long-term economic growth. So we have a convergence of two necessities: the kind of work environment which will bring self-fulfillment converging with the kind of workplace that is essential for long-term economic growth. How we manage the transition and cope with the change is critical.

Labor-management relations will either be characterized by consensus or confrontation. One of the things that will determine which it will be is how one answers the question those 15 million displaced manufacturing workers will ask: "What about me?" This means many different things. It means that workers and employees will have to become more effective as managers of the production process. It means that they will participate increasingly in management and ownership of companies. It means workers and management, together, will try to accomplish things that are in their mutual interest—things like greater productivity, quality improvement, cost savings. Every industry will have a different variation, whether it is quality-of-work life, membership on the board of directors, various forms of profit-sharing, or employee stock ownership plans that offer a true prospect of democratic capitalism.

The important point is not the specific suggestions, but that no such innovations can succeed unless management and labor are working as a team and treat these changes as opportunities and not as threats. I also happen to believe that one of the keys to that future is a new tax system that is much simpler, with lower rates of tax and far fewer tax loopholes. Such a system will encourage innovation and entrepreneurship and allow more rapid response to change. The challenge for labor-management relations is, in one sense, the same whatever the industry, but in another sense it is different, particularly for older industries. This is where I believe you have to take a look at some of the collective bargaining agreements that have been reached in autos, steel, and rubber in recent months and recent years, which indicate a framework that has yielded flexibility and, in my view, positive results. And I believe we have to build on that so that the

collective bargaining framework includes greater worker participation and future job security. The key is flexibility. For examples of a good and a bad way to proceed, let's take two cases
where there was a crisis in each industry in 1983. The companies
in crisis were Greyhound and Eastern. The way not to proceed
in my view is the way Greyhound proceeded which was to give
management very sizeable increases in wages and compensation
and then demand that the workers take a very big cut without
even a common agreement as to what was the crisis. Compare
that with Eastern Airlines where there was a dispute over what
was the crisis, but both sides agreed to have an outside individual
come in, analyze it, and then both sides agreed to take their
share of the sacrifice. The key here is shared sacrifice, shared
opportunity, and shared growth and profit. If you look at it
from a long-term point of view, this is the only way you put together a labor-management team that will endure and guarantee prosperity.

The history of United States labor-management relations
shows that, as soon as the winds of recession start to blow, workers are laid off. An exception that occurred in 1975, when Sony
took over a plant in Long Beach, California, is instructive. In
that 1975 recession, the new Sony management resisted the layoff process, and in the next year, productivity doubled. I am not
saying there was a direct cause and effect, but I would argue that
there was a relationship, and that more and more, we, as a society, have to recognize the value of our workers, and that their
long-term health will be determined, in part, by the health of the
company.

I believe those are the kinds of examples that will guide us
in the years to come. We are all on the cutting edge. I believe innovation and a caring society both are required for long-term
economic growth and prosperity. In one sense, we have had a
government that was concerned as it should be with minimal
economic benefits for those in our society who are elderly and
disadvantaged. But the times now require us also to be concerned about providing support to those citizens who have to adjust to rapid change. That is where I believe our work is critical.
*We are on the cutting edge of a change in the area of labor-management
relations.*

I believe what we do now and in the years ahead will determine whether we enter the twenty-first century as a productive and prosperous society, as one that has retained its self-respect, optimism and its belief that we still are, in addition to being individuals pursuing our own objectives, a community that is caring and mutually reinforcing.

Senator Bill Bradley

Part I

OVERVIEW

Chapter 1

LINKING WORKER PARTICIPATION WITH QUALITY AND EMPLOYMENT SECURITY

Sidney P. Rubinstein

Changing Assumptions

American industry will remain unprepared to compete effectively until certain basic assumptions now held by labor and management are abandoned. These assumptions relate specifically to the nature of productivity, worker participation, and quality. During the 1960s and 1970s, and continuing into the present, it generally has been assumed that the act of participation was sufficient, in itself, to provide the worker with the necessary motivation to perform effectively. Thus, the primary focus by industry was to encourage more and more of its workers to participate in the operations of the plant. What was not considered adequately was whether such participation produced results in solving some of the critical problems of productivity, quality, and competition.

Motivation stems from results, from the worker's success in solving the problems associated with his job. It does not arise from participation alone. Obviously, participation is necessary before the problem-solving process can be initiated—but the motivating force lies in the implemented solution. Only then does the worker acquire the sense of achievement and the feeling of self-actualization that gives impetus to creativity. A successful organization is one in which participative problem-solving is understood and remains the fundamental objective. To attain this objective requires changes in the way organizations currently are structured. This can be accomplished if the following changes take place:

- Establish the technical interface between various levels of employees that allows them to be effective problem-solvers;
- Modify conventional hierarchical and bureaucratic structures that tend to isolate one group from another;
- Bring people employed in different tasks and with differing skills into productive contact with each other: nontechnical workers with specialists and engineers; managers who have the responsibility for identifying and solving technical problems with workers who have line responsibility for producing the desired result.

It is not surprising that such restructuring should meet with opposition from both the union and middle management. It is difficult to alter the concepts and modalities that have become ingrained and part of the industrial mythology. For the most part, many unions still see themselves as reactive institutions, essentially protective agents in an adversarial role vis-à-vis management. In spite of enjoying an increasing measure of participation in various ways, they do not view themselves in a creative role — providing leadership in improving the methods and objectives of the particular operation in which they are engaged.

Even greater opposition to cooperative joint labor-management efforts to improve operations has been demonstrated by middle management. They have viewed such cooperation as a device to get them to support the demands of the workers. The engineers and technical staff, who are trained and organized in specialist departments, are reluctant to share their expertise and cooperate with workers, which they believe means sharing control of their technology.

It is difficult in a society such as ours, which has always viewed itself as preeminently successful in the economic sphere, to introduce basic changes in its industrial methods and philosophy. In the past, success meant the ability to mass produce products. The volume of the market and the volume of production was the critical basis for evaluation. In that era, everything that could be produced could be sold, because the capacity of the market was greater than the productive capacity. For this reason, industrial plants were designed to produce according to quantitative and not qualitative objectives. When concepts of scientific management were introduced into the design of the production process, control shifted to the technically trained staffs. Engineers began designing the process and setting the standards. Middle management, which in the past had performed both functions now turned over their authority in this area to the technical staffs and concentrated on supervising the operation and its people.

Managers, who previously had quality control responsibility, now had quality control staffs setting the standards and inspecting the process. Managers who used to determine the rate of production now had industrial engineers making the determination. Those who used to deal with personnel problems now had personnel specialists working for them. A bureaucratic organization developed which depended on obedience. Each level of management was expected to be obedient to a higher level. And the whole organization was expected to be obedient to the methods, standards and procedures established by the specialist department.

This also produced a change in the status of the work force. Production workers were assumed to have only minimal skills: they could be hired and trained quickly for the production process. For the same reason, they could be laid off quickly. Because they were assumed to have only minimal skills it was believed that no great loss resulted from their departure: new workers could be quickly hired and trained to replace them.

Foremen became primarily supervisory people but were not involved in the planning process or in challenging methodology. Unions were organized primarily to counteract the arbitrary behavior of management when it violated the workers' sense of fairness with regard to compensation or how they were being treated at the workplace. This system, which evolved at the turn of the century and dominated production through World War II, was deemed extremely effective compared with earlier methods. It was deemed a great success, as indeed it was.

In general, the history of modern industry is one in which technological advances, combined with scientific management and the rationalization of work itself, led to vast increases in productivity. In return for these advances in productivity, the industrial system lost its ability to generate workers with skills and decision-making capacity. The same loss occurred in management relative to their own skills. Rationalization of management functions led to rivalries within management over knowledge and authority, as well as conflict among workers, inspectors, and supervisors over decision-making.

Following World War II, the rapidly growing market encouraged companies to continue operating along these bureaucratic lines. It encouraged the unions to fight for higher compensation and more benefits. It encouraged the specialist departments to flourish, popularizing the need for specialized training and leading to more people entering the specialist field.

This model was deemed successful until two major events took place. First, the opening of educational opportunities for the returning serviceman became the trigger for changing the attitudes, values, and expectations of the work force. The people who joined the work force were now high school graduates, whereas in the prior generation, most people did not finish grade school. Today, the supervisor is frequently a college graduate, whereas in the past he may have finished high school.

In every area, a higher level of education encouraged higher expectations. People were now looking for more control and influence over their own work experience. But they quickly discovered that they had entered a work environment which was restrictive, undemocratic, and a dead end.

In their private lives many of these people were active in civic, religious, and school organizations where they engaged in policy-level decision-making. At home, they were also making decisions and solving problems related to finances, consumer choices, health care, and electing their representatives. But when they went to the workplace, they often were treated like children with no input in solving the problems that arose in their work areas. When they made efforts to solve such problems, they met with opposition. It is not surprising that they also were discouraged.

These changes in the expectations of the work force were accelerated further by the various social movements then taking place throughout the country on behalf of civil rights, civil liberties, anti-Vietnam protests, and similar activities. All of these forces combined to produce a ferment among many workers —young and old—who realized that they had the capacity of making a greater contribution than the restrictions of the job permitted. Out of this feeling of frustration emerged a sense of alienation—the "blue-collar blues." The worker believed he was prevented from participating in matters that were not only appropriate to his function but important to his self-image.

The second phenomenon was that a country that had been devastated by World War II lifted itself out of the ashes with American help and became the leading quality producer of many products of the world. Japan achieved this position by changing the way it organized its industry and establishing new relationships between labor and management, between the worker and his workplace, and between the managers themselves. In addition, the new system did not rely on the specialist. Technical knowledge and skills were made accessible to all workers. It was a fundamental change in the methods of organizing production.

Awareness of the new worker has been with us for more than 30 years. I was personally in a position to recognize the changing nature of the work force as far back as the early 1950s when I spent six years working as a machinist and tool-and-die maker. It soon became clear to me that the people in the shops around me had great capabilities, a spirit of confidence, and considerable know-how. They also experienced great frustration because their competence was not being fully utilized.

At a later period, I had the experience of working as an engineer and being told by engineering management, "Don't ask the workers how to solve your problems because that implies that we engineers don't know how to solve them." The readiness of the work force to take on more complex tasks was already apparent in the 1950s.

The Evolution of Participative Systems

A strong theoretical foundation exists for participative systems. Since the 1920s, behavioral scientists have been identifying the various motivational needs of the individual: the social needs of belonging, which can be fulfilled through the process of participation; the ego needs, which require a sense of recognition and responsibility; the need for self-actualization, which can be met through opportunities for creativity and problem-solving. It has been pointed out that in order to fulfill these needs, it is vital to reorganize the nature and conditions of working life. Only in this way can industry avoid a sense of widespread alienation and dissatisfaction at the workplace.

In this same period, the engineering community developed simple, industrial engineering and statistical quality control methods which can be used by workers and supervisors to solve problems.

Linking Employee Participation and Quality Control

In 1959, after having been trained in statistics and quality control, I became a consultant with the assignment to introduce quality control in a small (corrugated container) plant. There, I organized a problem-solving team of workers which included the foremen and union stewards of the department. They demonstrated a high degree of competence and enthusiasm. Very rapidly, a whole series of quality problems were solved. That was the beginning of my experience in organizing teams of workers and supervisors to work on quality problems, which has been an ongoing process ever since. Between 1959–1971 this activity was known as Participative Quality Control and was implemented in more than 40 plants in the paper, corrugated container, envelope, and small assembly industries by S.P. Rubinstein Associates. In addition to problem-solving, the focus was on introducing greater self-control, changing the role of inspectors and enabling the operators of the machines to assume their own inspection responsibilities.

The biggest frustration during that period was returning to the plant after two years to find that very little of the process still remained. It seemed that, unless there was someone actively interested and supportive, the process would come apart. In early projects, survival depended heavily on the continued involvement of the consultant. By 1970, I realized that a system had to be created which would involve the commitment of management and labor, have an organizational structure which would be ongoing, and would allow for management and labor participation at various levels of the organization. It could not depend for its success only on the outstanding manager or consultant.

The problem-solving teams which had evolved were similar in design to the Japanese quality control circles (QC circles). Most of these projects lasted between two and four years. In looking back, it was clear that Participative Quality Control was only a *partial* system without the integrated organizational elements needed for continuity. However, it was useful in demonstrating that workers *could* and *did solve* quality problems effectively; that their motivation increased in proportion to the amount of control they had over their operations; and that a structured system including internal coordinators was needed to sustain the initial program and train new teams.

A System for the Whole Organization

After returning from the first International Quality Control Conference in Japan in 1969, I shifted the focus from Participative Quality Control, which concentrated on involving workers in the quality function, to Participative Problem Solving®, which provided the concepts and skills for all members of an organization to participate in improving all functions. This broader concept was what I saw operating in Japan. In the words of Kaoru Ishikawa:

> QC in Japan is characterized by company-wide participation, from the top management to the employees. It is actively participated in not only by the departments of tech-

nology, design, research, and manufacturing, but also by sales, materials, clerical or managerial departments, such as planning, accounting, business, and personnel.[1]

The United States needed a similar concept. The first step was to develop training materials to train the coordinator/trainers inside the plant who, in turn, would train the workers, supervisors and managers in the new systems. To this purpose, Participative Systems, Inc. was organized in 1971 as a training and consulting firm.

A New Role for the Union

The first training of coordinator/trainers was in the printing industry in 1972. The trade union, Amalgamated Lithographers, Local 1, represents the lithographic workers in the New York area. We were asked to train its staff in the concepts and methods of Participative Problem-Solving® so that they, in turn, could train their apprentices to use these methods in the various plants where they were working. This project helped us realize the tremendous added potential that came with the interest and support of the union. As participative systems continued to develop, so did the related quality of work life field.

Initiating Quality of Work Life

In the 1970s, Irving Bluestone, former vice president of the United Auto Workers and director of the General Motors Department of the UAW, was the principal leader of the quality of work life (QWL) movement in the auto industry. In describing some of its objectives, he declared:

> The worker should experience genuinely that he is not simply an adjunct to the tool, but that his bents toward being creative, innovative, inventive, and to play an active role in the production or service should be acknowledged. [He] should be assured that [taking part] in decision-making will not erode his job security or that of his fellow workers.
>
> We must democratize the workplace so that the worker

can enjoy . . . a measure of the democratic values he enjoys
as a citizen of a democratic country.[2]

As a result of Bluestone's ideas and his ability to convince both
the UAW and GM to experiment with QWL, the process went
forward.

A pioneering formal joint labor-management commitment
in the United States came when General Motors and the United
Auto Workers agreed to start their quality of work life process in
1973. Their collective bargaining agreement that year provided
for a national joint committee to improve the quality of work
life. The parties agreed to urge local managements and local
unions to cooperate in quality of work life experiments and projects. I was asked to serve as the consultant to the first project under this agreement.

A participative problem-solving process was set up as a formal pilot project and training program in the Tarrytown, New
York assembly plant of General Motors, guided by a joint labor-
management committee. The top leaders of the union and the
management agreed to a set of guidelines which included these
points:

- participation would be voluntary;
- no provisions of the national or local collective bargaining agreements would be violated;
- either party could withdraw from the program at any
  time;
- a union leader and an engineer were selected as joint
  coordinators of the OWL pilot program.

We trained the initial pilot teams at the plant for 40 hours in
Participative Problem Solving®. This course was planned to enhance the ability of teams and individuals to solve the problems
that confronted them daily. The two greatest assets that they
possessed for solving these problems were their common sense
and experience. In recognition of this, the program focused primarily on making them examine and evaluate the reasoning
processes they habitually used to solve problems and on intro-

ducing new methods available to improve these processes. The emphasis was on learning by experience; that is, by participating in problem-solving activity and then evaluating the experience. A significant innovation consisted of the effort spent on puzzles and demonstration problems. Through this process of solving abstract problems, they learned concepts, tools, and methods which can be effectively applied to the problem-solving process for real problems.

The content of the course included the following areas:

- Participative Problem Solving® concepts;
- Building a team;
- Understanding a problem;
- Problem-solving strategies;
- Testing, implementing, and evaluating;
- Administrative needs.

This form of education captured the enthusiasm of the workers by establishing a sense of equality within the group for it did not depend on prior academic education.

The specially selected puzzles produced excellent analogies to various systems problems. For example, a puzzle called "Decision Points" is very useful for identifying points in the manufacturing process that seriously affect the outcome. A review of how workers do their jobs and why they select a particular way to do them frequently reveals important "Decision Points," as in the following example:

> Five members of the team worked at applying urethane to the windshields. The team decided to focus on their operation when they determined that windshield leakers were a critical defect. Urethane is both the sealer and adhesive that holds the windshield in the body of the car. The workers used a urethane applicator to extrude by hand a bead of urethane along the edge of the windshield. The windshield was then placed in the body of the car. We asked each worker to describe his method of applying urethane. The first worker reported that he applied the urethane starting at the upper right-hand corner because he was right-handed,

and it was easier for him. The others started at different points on the perimeter for different reasons. The fifth worker was at first reluctant to describe his method. With some coaxing by the team, he reported that he started 10 inches from the right-hand corner at the bottom. The windshield had an antenna sealed in the glass, and the leads protrude 10 inches from the right-hand corner. This worker had determined that the windshield leaks occurred primarily at this point, where the water could run down along the wires. By starting the urethane application at this point and ending at this point, an excessive amount would be deposited, causing a dam that prevented the leaks. This worker had used his relief periods to observe the water test operation. He noticed that, most of the time, leaks occurred at the same point, where the leads came out of the windshield. Data was available each day on the number of leaks, but not where the leaks occurred. He had changed his own method, but had not shared his findings with the foreman or the other people in the department. There had not been any encouragement in the past for workers to share such information. The creation of the problem-solving team changed that environment. This worker's recommendation was tested and accepted as the most effective method by the whole team. The team redesigned the water test report, using the diagram of the windshield to show where it leaked, as well as the number of leaks. This new information led to other improvements in the process by other workers. The teams almost completely eliminated leakers, and their methods were adopted by other assembly plants.

Many quality problems were solved by the pilot teams. One of the consequences of the pilot program was that some of the workers acquired a good deal of influence. Because of their knowledge and ability, management had to consider their proposals seriously. Management, however, was reluctant to have a formal program that was so structured as to commit superintendents and general foremen in department advisory committees to meet with workers and problem-solving teams and respond to the workers' recommendations. They were reluctant to appear to give the workers too much power. Subsequently, the plant labor-management committee substituted a communication training progam for the problem-solving training provided in the pilot and delivered it to 95 percent of the plant. It focused on the principal concern of the company and the union—to improve labor-management relations. The desire to involve the entire plant was, in this way, realized, and the results were impressive. Factors that are affected by the shop floor environment and the relationships between supervisors and the workers improved greatly, especially grievances and absenteeism, which went down sharply. The change in attitudes improved Tarrytown's position in the comparative quality index among assembly plants; technical and quality problems which could effectively be solved by shop floor teams were rarely addressed by the workers, however. These problems remained in the exclusive domain of management, engineering, and specialist functions. The frustration felt by Tarrytown workers who were not organized to solve problems after their exposure to QWL communications training was not documented and reported. Improved relations was considered enough. To have workers solve problems, they needed an organizational structure and the willingness of management and technical departments to share information. This would have been a more complex model that, for the most part, has still not been developed in many companies that maintain the QWL process.

The Tarrytown project received much publicity, and the principles it incorporated became well-known and utilized. It was outstanding in setting a precedent for developing joint labor-management programs, even though it fell short of significantly involving the workers in problem-solving. Nevertheless, it was a necessary step in the process of reducing bitter, adversarial relationships between the union and management. Those programs which followed attempted to duplicate the principles of the pilot program. Most did not follow the communication training model, however.

Organizational elements of the pilot which affected labor-management relations were maintained, including:

- the labor-management policy committee, which brought, for the first time, non-adversarial contact between the

chairman of the grievance committee and the plant manager and production manager;
- equality in administration with union and management coordinators, and
- shop floor teams.

The department advisory committee, which was discontinued after the pilot program, was not included.

A two-tier system, with the plant policy committee being seen as an administrative body to the teams, was promoted as the organization model. For a long time it was believed that an adequate QWL structure requires only a plant steering committee, labor-management coordinators, and shop floor teams.

This organizational structure was not effective in developing support by middle management. Top management accepted the process but middle managers and some of the department-level union leadership had legitimate problems with the concept.

A major breakthrough would require that we define and resolve two major issues. The system had to help middle management deal with their own needs for security and motivation, as well as the problems of productivity and quality for which they were responsible. In addition, a proper approach toward productivity and quality was required, to which the union leadership could respond. Tarrytown is the longest ongoing quality of work life process. Its contribution to the field has been invaluable. Workers, managers and union leaders have endured the ups and downs, and have adjusted their process based on their own assessment and creativity. It is reported that they are now focused on problem-solving.

From Pilot Programs to Total Plant Systems

In the late 1970s, we provided consultation and training for many total plant projects. This included labor-management support systems and problem-solving teams in all departments. Total plant systems were installed in the stamping, brass, auto assembly, glass, shipbuilding, copier, electric, steel fabricating, telephone, aerospace, and other industries, with varying degrees of success.

Training programs were developed for senior management and union leaders. Joint plant-level policy committees were created whereby union leadership and management together developed policy statements identifying common goals and operating principles. They also developed plans for the implementation of their system and arranged for resources and follow-up. In many locations where the process began in a highly adversarial environment, the parties soon learned to work together effectively, with a high degree of enthusiasm.

The training of the coordinator/trainers proved to be effective. Teams could be trained easily and organized to solve various work area problems. High return on these projects quickly followed in the form of improvement in quality and productivity.

What continued to cause difficulty was the review process with the superintendents and middle management. In many cases, the superintendents and general foremen continued to resist their involvement and resented having to give time to the teams. We tried to develop a number of models to overcome this problem.

But these advisory committees were still having difficulty meeting on a regular basis. They provided poor guidance to the teams who would frequently focus on problems that were insignificant to members of the advisory group.

It finally was determined that instead of asking middle management to support the teams, a method had to be developed whereby the teams could support middle management and help it deal with the problems of productivity and quality. Middle management and the technical staff feel responsible for quality and will encourage team support and assistance on such problems. At the same time, we had to relate productivity and quality to employment security. This formulation the union leadership found attractive.

Entering the Third Stage

Participative Systems has now entered its third stage. In the first stage the system focused on workers, involving and training

them in self-control (operator inspection and process adjust-
ment) and problem-solving. In the second stage, it focused on
changing relationships between labor and management and developing joint labor-management cooperation. The focus was on
the senior plant-level union leaders and managers, as well as on
the shop floor relationship between workers and supervisors. In
the third stage, sanctioned by new collective bargaining agreements, the parties developed a joint labor-management consultative process focused on developing an integrated social and
technical system. This system stresses employment stability and
improving productivity and quality. The consultative process
goes beyond cooperation with a structure, authority and responsibility for all parties.

On August 1, 1980 one of the most significant new labor
agreements was negotiated between the United Steelworkers of
America and the major steel corporations. It included the following paragraphs:

> The parties recognize that a cooperative approach between
> employees and supervision at the work site in a department
> or similar unit is essential to the solution of problems affect-
> ing them. Many problems at this level are not readily sub-
> ject to resolution under existing contractual programs and
> practices, but affect the ongoing relationships between la-
> bor and management at that level. Joint participation in
> solving these problems at the department level is an essen-
> tial ingredient in any effort to improve the effectiveness of
> the company's performance and to provide employees with
> a measure of involvement adding dignity and worth to their
> work life.
>
> A participation team shall be free to discuss, consider
> and decide upon proposed means to improve department
> or unit performance, employee morale and dignity, and
> conditions of the work site. Appropriate subjects among
> others which a team might consider would include: use of
> production facilities; quality of product and quality of the
> work environment; safety and environmental health;
> scheduling and reporting arrangements; absenteeism and

overtime; incentive coverage and yield; job alignment; contracting out; energy conservation and transportation pools. . .[3]

This contract provided greater impetus and a more specific mandate to the cooperative labor-management effort. The first Labor-Management Participation Team (LMPT) programs for which we acted as consultants were launched at two US Steel mills near Pittsburgh. At one of them, the Edgar Thomson mill (ongoing LMPT process since 1981), a statement was issued by the labor-management policy committee which captured the new spirit: "The relationships and the beneficial process of working together to solve problems of common interest leads to making all of us better as workers and as managers. That, in turn, will help to make Edgar Thomson a more productive, efficient steelmaking plant which leads to more employment security and better working conditions."[4]

It was made clear that involvement in these participative teams would be voluntary. The plant labor-management committee agreed not only to administer the system but also to serve as a problem-solving team at its own level. This process helped to create both a sense of accomplishment and a sense of participation. It also provided an example for the work force as a whole which resulted in a large number of volunteers and great interest in LMPT participation.

At the Irvin mill, the plant management and union leadership viewed the program in their plant as a pilot project that would become a model for the company, union, and industry. The economic recession in the steel industry at that time provided the stimulus to maximize the effectiveness of the LMPT process. Both labor and management were willing to break new ground and find answers to persistent problems.

There were two important breakthroughs that took place simultaneously. A method for planning significant projects at the department level was created, as well as a plan for employment stability. The key was the creation of project planning subcommittees of the department advisory committee. We developed this concept after a series of interviews with general foremen, and found that they were frustrated that they were not able to solve many of the problems important to them. One general foreman spent two to three hours per day handling the problems of defective materials, specifically coils that had been rejected. He, however, had no time to spend in solving problems that would *prevent* materials from being defective. The other general foremen had similar experiences. In discussions with top management, it became clear that it was highly desirable that a new process be developed, one that would assist general foremen and superintendents to effectively improve their operations.

The first subcommittee for managing projects was organized with one general foreman, one quality control metallurgist, and the union grievanceman representing the particular area. As a consequence, these three men from the cold reduction department were relieved of their other responsibilities by operators and supervisors so they could meet for a period of 2–4 hours a day, one day a week, on a continuing basis. At the No. 2–5 Stand cold reduction mill, they began identifying various types of problems—problems dealing with materials from other departments; problems inherent in their own operations; and problems that were inadvertently passed on to the next department.

In a few weeks, not only were the problems identified, they were broken down into workable dimensions. The three men worked as a planning and problem-solving team, providing solutions themselves. In some instances, the problems were assigned to technical support people. The shop-floor teams also agreed to solve related problems. In this way, we were able to provide new insights for management on how to plan and organize efforts for improvement which were more complex and time consuming than the problems a shop-floor team can tackle.

The subcommittee introduced many innovative concepts directed toward establishing a more stable work force. For example, six workers were recalled from layoff to fill in, allowing other workers with relevant knowledge to devote their full-time to implementing solutions. The senior mill roller was thereby freed to do the initial assessment of the machine changes needed. This was the first time a production worker performed this function. Four maintenance workers were able to implement machine changes. A special program was devised to train the work crew. One production employee per week, on a rotation basis, received extensive training in quality problems and procedures. He, too, was replaced in his regular job by a worker recalled from layoff.

At the conclusion of the program, the senior executive responsible for steel operations reported on the work of the subcommittee and the three labor-management shop-floor teams.

> Now, let me describe a team project at U.S. Steel's Irvin Works undertaken to improve the productivity and the quality of the No. 2–5 Stand cold reduction mill.
>
> Four separate LMPTs tackled four different aspects of the problem.
>
> The heart of the problem was with the rolling solution system which is a critical part of the cold reduction process.
>
> The rolling solution is 96 percent water; a viscosity that is important in terms of the solution interacting with the various machinery and the strip steel product.
>
> In the course of their problem-solving, the LMPT identified nine areas which had to be corrected in order to revise the solution system and increase efficiency.
>
> I'll omit the details, but all nine of the recommendations of the team have been adopted at a total cost for labor and materials of $86,700. The savings on an annual basis . . . over $500,000.
>
> Those savings are attained through:
>
> • Improvement in the quality;
> • A reduction in the amount of rolling oil solution needed;
> • Reduced downtime on the mill.
>
> In terms of operating performance . . . in a base period prior to the changes . . . the mill averaged 91.5 percent of standard. Since the changes . . . the unit has maintained an operating performance of slightly more than 100 percent. And in one month, it exceeded 111 percent.

> The problems of a lesser nature identified and cor-
> rected by the other teams bring the total savings on the No.
> 2–5 Stand to over $600,000 per year.[5]

The creation of a structured planning and problem-solving capability at the department level, which could provide project management, had a highly desirable organizational effect. Other departments organized advisory subcommittees with similar results in solving important problems and providing employment for additional workers who would otherwise be laid off.

Seeing effective project management functioning well with new planners helped us reach the following conclusion. Perhaps the most disastrous effect of the Taylor system is the creation of middle management without effective authority, influence and credibility. Most of the managers are operating well below their capacity, concentrating on supervising and fire fighting without time for planning and problem-solving. The new system expanded the authority and influence, and reduced the stress and frustration of the general foreman and the quality control metallurgist. This reduced considerably the traditional antagonism between operational management and staff functions. Equally important, it provided a new role for the union grievanceman. With grievances declining he now has a cost-effective method of attacking a new concern, namely avoiding layoffs. In addition, people who had been laid off could be brought back to implement improvements or be trained for new functions. Shifting the role of union and management department leadership from primarily administrative functions with regard to employee participation to planning, coordinating and problem-solving has created the operating conditions for the next stage: a coordinated organization-wide system.

The lessons learned from the Irvin experience have influenced the development of participative systems. Because the LMPT process at Irvin was suspended after 2 years, the workers and managers involved have received little recognition. The union and management were not adequately prepared to protect this success. Policies generated because of the economic crisis caused a strong adversarial response. LMPT became a bargaining chip in unsuccessful negotiations on local issues, while support from the international was suspended during a crisis with the corporation. For such systems to survive, labor and management must learn how to protect and sustain advances in joint efforts during periods when they are battling on adversarial issues.

A Total System

Here, in essence, is the microcosm of a total, integrated Participative System, providing for employment security, effective quality control, and the proper utilization of human resources, including middle management. It counteracted the problem of alienation by giving each level of operation—the shop floor, middle management, and the specialist group—the sense of authority, participation and personal accomplishment essential to improve quality and increase productivity.

Its application to employment security and stabilized employment was self-evident in its use of additional manpower in a number of departments to release workers for problem-solving activities, and other workers for special training in relevant areas. It also provided release time for the union representatives, the general foremen and other supervisory and technical personnel to plan and administer the program.

The initial projects made it possible to draw certain basic conclusions:

- Union leadership welcomed the training in special skills, planning and problem-solving;
- Middle management, specifically the superintendent and general foreman, could effectively participate in planning committees composed of both technical staff and union leadership;
- Employment security, productivity, and quality improvement could be mutual objectives, and cooperating teams could now be organized at all levels of the plant including the shop floor, department level man-

agement, and union leadership, as well as plant level senior managers and union officers;
- Shop-floor teams welcomed input and guidance from advisory committees. They wanted to work on important problems.

These principles have since been developed fully and applied in a number of industries. The experiences at the Iron and Steel Division of Interlake, Inc. and Ethicon Inc., a Johnson & Johnson company, discussed in following chapters, are excellent examples of advanced systems.

The system consists of three primary levels of teams as shown in Figure 1-1. At the plant-wide level is a policy committee made up of top management and union officers. This group is responsible for setting organizational priorities, planning the process, setting policy, administering the program, and solving problems of a plant-wide nature.

The second level is the department advisory committee for each major department, division, or function. This level is composed of middle management, union representatives, and relevant staff and technical service functions. Their responsibilities include developing detailed plans to meet organizational objectives. Subcommittees are frequently formed for directing improvement projects, communicating, supporting, and coordinating the activities of the individual problem-solving teams. Advisory committees are also problem-solving groups at the department level.

The third level is the individual problem-solving team of employees and supervisors.

The Contrast With Japan

The essence of the Japanese experience has been the full utilization of all human resources in a continuing process of improving productivity and quality. It is a system backed by much of the society—based on a new social relationship. Labor was invited to participate in the movement, and management committed itself to working for stable employment and employment security. The government committed itself to support the entire effort.

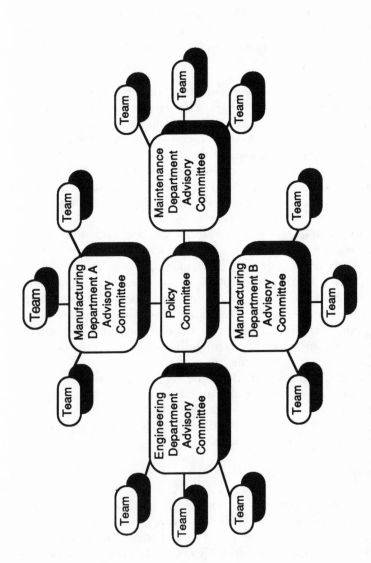

Figure 1-1.   Participative Systems labor/management structure for manufacturing

This new social contract led to the discovery of new relationships at the workplace.

> In order to cope with the many changes, both domestic and foreign which have affected Japan's economy so drastically, the improvement of productivity in all fields of national endeavor is essential for the achievement of a healthy and stable economy.
>
> The first Productivity Liaison Conference, held on May 21, 1955 and attended by representatives from government, labor, and management, adopted the Three Guiding Principles which summarized their understanding of the nature and purpose of the productivity movement as follows:
>
> 1. In the long run, improvement in productivity will increase employment. However, during the transition, before the full effects of improved productivity have yet become apparent, the government and the people, in order to minimize temporary frictions which may disturb the national economy, must cooperate to provide suitable measures, such as the transferring of surplus workers to areas where needed, in order to prevent unemployment.
> 2. In developing concrete measures to increase productivity, labor and management, conforming to the conditions existing in the respective enterprises, must cooperate in discussing, studying and deliberating such measures.
> 3. The fruits of improved productivity must, in correspondence with the condition of the national economy, be distributed fairly among management, labor and the consumer.[6]

In the environment created by this social contract, the conditions for a new labor-management quality system evolved. I have described the conditions as follows:

> This integrated social and technical system requires a supportive environment, which has been created through spe-

cial social relations in the workplace involving personnel policies (shared benefits such as employment security), management style (consensus management), and labor relations (union-management joint consultation and joint planning at the shop floor, plant, and corporate levels).[7]

Training became vital to the procedure. Workers were transferred from agricultural areas and trained to become industrial workers. To obtain a full return on the investment in training, workers were encouraged to become permanent employees. The opportunity for employment security encouraged training and led to quality improvement. It enabled many companies, after each recession, to be more effective in capturing a larger share of the market. This closed loop was self-supporting: training produced quality; quality produced market; market produced employment security.

The critical test occurred in 1973 when Japan experienced its first major downturn in the economy since the development of the joint labor-management consultation agreements. The commitments were lived up to. Instead of laying off its surplus employees, industry maintained their employment, shifted employees to new job assignments, expanded the problem-solving activity and training process and emerged from the downturn with higher levels of quality and productivity than ever before. Employment security was provided to permanent workers, managers, and staff.

Through this system Japanese industry was able to capture new markets during the period of post-recession growth, whereas American industry had laid its people off and, when the recession ended, had to recall many of them. Many would not come back; that meant recruiting workers and retraining them. The consequence was that it took considerable time to restore productivity to pre-recession levels.

The Japanese have discovered that employment security is the key to getting a competitive edge on the market. And the key to employment security is an organized system of planning alternatives, such as training workers who would otherwise be laid off during a recession. In contrast, the prevailing practice in American companies is that they can lay off people and make society responsible for their welfare. Apart from the burden on society, there is the additional loss of valuable experience and skills.

Explicit Joint Department Leadership

Today, there is considerable evidence that middle management and staff people find themselves in an insecure and non-rewarding position. They are overworked and underutilized, with very little opportunity for creativity and growth. The reverse is true in Japan because they do not have the vast array of specialist departments of quality control, personnel, etc. The staff is better utilized and middle managers perform many of these functions themselves. They exercise greater authority in problem-solving and have closer relationhips with the workers. They have more time for planning and creative problem-solving. One major difference is that, in Japan, the foreman is frequently a member of the union, and many middle managers are former officers of the union, giving them greater credibility with the worker. Therefore, labor-management joint consultation at the department level is implicit, because the foreman and the department manager are exercising the role of leadership in organizing the work and solving personal, social, and technical problems.

We have seen top management in American industry interested in change. But middle managers have resisted because they have seen no alternative in which they would be more effective. We have seen labor mistakenly believe that good communication with top management will change the behavior of middle management and supervisors.

What we now find is the need for labor to be directly involved in planning and solving problems in cooperation with specialists and middle managers. The strength of the labor leaders at the local level who represent their workers is a key element in developing more effective management and leadership at the department level. The organization in the United States, at this level, will not be able to be implicit like that in Japan. Differences in history, the role of the union, and culture require an explicit joint consultative process. The mechanism for doing this is a multilevel system of joint labor-management committees at all existing levels.

The organizational structure of mature mass production industries in the United States following the Taylor system has developed into the "machine bureacracy." "The machine bureaucracy is a structure with an obsession—namely, control. A control mentality pervades it from top to bottom."[8] Obedience is demanded and expected from all. This is particularly true among levels of management. Bureaucratized industries cannot compete with newly organized mass production industries that focus on consensus management, creativity, and continued quality improvement. To encourage the development of this kind of organization, an environment must be created which provides for the freedom to challenge, freedom to disagree with peers and supervisors, freedom to experiment, and freedom to show initiative.

This freedom can only exist and prosper in a democratic environment where authority is shared and present in a number of forms:

- Citizenship provides the authority and responsibility to the individual to decide and control his own action;
- Participative democracy comes from authority delegated to the work team for problem-solving and decision-making;
- Representative democracy: At the department, plant, and company levels, provides legal rights and authority at the policy level.

A stable system requires all three types of democratic authority. The periodic conflict, when splitting the pie, produces a normal and desirable adversarial relationship. Collective bargaining between legal representatives of labor and management allows for the resolution of this conflict through negotiations or actions between parties with equal authority. This sense of equality helps the parties put aside their adversarial feelings once an agreement has been reached. The environment for citizenship and participative democracy can thereby flourish.

The evidence is not yet conclusive, but there is reason to believe that the systems will tend to be unstable in companies which are implementing participative democracy (QC circles) without representative democracy (unions). Unilateral actions by management deemed as unfair can negate the environment where people will be interested in *volunteering* their energy and their time to actively participate in their organization. Also, department and plant committees with employee representatives may be in violation of current labor laws.

The strengths and weaknesses characteristic in the traditional management system is paralleled in the union hierarchy and within the staff functions. Our planning and problem-solving teams are of common interest to the three primary institutional groups at work: management, technical and professional staff, and labor union representatives and employees. The authority of each team is based on the authority of each of its members within their hierarchical institution. The focus of each team is based on the function, area, or level of responsibility of its principal members. These levels have legitimacy, competence, and motivation because they are based on the participation of all three institutional groups. Such a restructuring creates a new social system in the workplace based on equality of input and common objectives. Thus, social needs, as well as business needs, are fulfilled.

The multi-level explicit labor-management consultative process has now been developed in the United States. It is the functional equivalent of the company-wide quality control and the labor-management consultative process in Japan.

Quality Control

The impact of this system on quality control is quite clear. The hierarchical and specialist quality system is effective in planning, setting standards, evaluating, and reporting results. However, it is not competitive in enabling operators to assume responsibilities and to control the process, thereby eliminating the necessity of inspectors and overseers. It is particularly ineffective in advancing the rate of quality improvement. This rate is adversely affected by the misuse of human resources. Because problems are solved only by managers and specialists, the resources available are limited and, therefore, the only problems which receive a problem-solving focus are those few which are defined as critical. Problems should be assigned to non-specialists who are able to solve them with their adequate technical knowledge, so the those with specialized knowledge can focus on those problems that require technical expertise. If problems are assigned to quality specialists and engineers, which can better be solved using the operating expertise and knowledge of workers or supervisors, a misapplication of resources takes place. The multilevel system is precisely what is required to properly identify quality objectives and priorities and to properly assign problems to those best capable of solving them. It frees those with greater skills to solve the more complex problems.

There are three current trends in the field of quality control in the United States today which need to be assessed:

1. Quality as a management function;
2. Expanded use of statistical quality control;
3. Q.C. circles.

These trends are open to question as to their ability to make the American production system competitive in terms of quality in the world market. Senior quality control consultants like J.M. Juran are pessimistically viewing the progress of American industry in becoming competitive in quality:

> We are making improvements in some industries at an unprecedented pace. But up to now the pace hasn't been good enough. The gap's too big. And for that reason I'm pretty sure that gap is not going to be closed in this decade. We have to work at it more energetically than we have been, and particularly redesign our approaches so that every year without fail we can make improvements at a rapid pace— what I call institutionalizing improvements. In the main that has not been done yet. We still have that to do.[9]

Many influential consultants see the quality system as primarily a management responsibility. Management and technical personnel provide the motivation and direction for the system. Managers are encouraged to form quality-oriented problem-solving teams in addition to performing traditional functions.

Without a system that provides for redistribution of responsibilities at all levels of the organization—involving greater responsibilities for the worker and supervisor at every level—managers will not have the available time to effectively be involved in problem-solving. They only can have enough time if the other responsibilities they now exercise are assumed at a lower level. Many of these problems have to be solved by workers and supervisors, where there is both the interest, the resources and the knowledge to solve them. Most important, there is little commitment to solving the quality problems if the entire basis of analyzing and assessing the results of the quality system is solely cost effectiveness and rate of failure. The social objectives of employment security and equality at the workplace must be considered to establish the quality objective as the means and strategic unifying goal of modern organizations. It is particularly unfortunate when management unilaterally imposes a quality improvement program in an organization where a labor-management joint consultative process can be organized, for the two systems will often be in competition and conflict.

A rebirth of interest is now occurring in the United States in statistical quality control. This system was developed by American scientists and engineers in the early 1940s. Statistical quality control is a set of tools based on simple statistical techniques which are highly useful in process control and operations improvement. Although statistical quality control techniques are rooted in more sophisticated statistical analysis, they were developed so that they could be easily taught to technical personnel and production foremen and workers, thereby providing simple scientific tools for quality control and improvement. To disseminate these methods to the broadest popular audience, a strenuous broad-based effort was launched. In the early 1950s, many major firms were actively involved in educating their foremen and workers in statistical quality control. The organizational environment, however, was not prepared to accept foremen or workers in quality or productivity improvement. Some engineers and foremen misunderstood the use of control charts and interpreted the indications on the chart meaning that a process was out of control as the basis for criticizing the operator and his performance.

Statistical quality control was often assigned to specialists.

This grew out of the prevailing philosophy of scientific management, which supported the trend toward more specialists and specialized departments. We can surmise that popular use by foremen and workers of statistical methodology will take root only when it is part of a total integrated social and technical system. In my opinion, what the workers and unions rejected in the 1950s and 1960s was not statistical quality control but the quality management system. In many firms where this statistical quality control education is again being introduced, it is occurring without the development of a supportive social environment or integrated technical system. As things now stand, this effort will be seen as a *partial* system, and will not endure in spite of the current interest of management.

The introduction of statistical quality control through the multi-level system provides a realistic opportunity to institutionalize the use of statistical methodology at all levels of the organization because there is both a social and a technical support system encouraging that development. In current projects, labor as well as management is encouraging the use of statistical quality control at all levels.[10]

The quality control circle movement, which in the United States has developed as a unilateral management system, has placed the creation of quality circles as an end in itself. This movement has already experienced a high rate of failure—and it is likely that this will continue. What we hope will come out of this experience is that managers and unions will be influenced by the willingness of workers to be involved in quality control circles. They will recognize that the absence of an integrated social/technical support system results in failure, lack of support and discontinuity. It is to be hoped that they will seek to restructure their organization to fully utilize the human resources and the interests of the worker.

Labor-Management Quality Control

In the application of the multilevel system to the quality control function, organizations have found a number of transitional stages. To increase the rate of quality improvement they can evaluate how supervisors, middle managers and union leadership are now using their time. If adequate time is not available for participation in the problem-solving and planning process, and assessment should be made as to what tasks can be undertaken by others at a lower level of authority in the organization. Thus, the opportunities derived from the multilevel problem-solving process become available.

The participants at all levels should seriously access the problems they are solving or selecting. Table 1-1 describes guidelines for assigning resources for solving problems. This evaluation is based on the nature of the problem and on the qualifications of each group. This differs from a traditional quality control system. By assigning "on-line" problems to supervisors and workers, more time is available for management and the technical staff to work on "off-line" problems. A similar result took place in Japan and was reported by Professor Yoshio Kondo:

> Thus the engineers and staffs can entrust to the foremen and workers, without any worry, the greatest part of their daily jobs as trouble shooters, and they can concentrate their efforts on . . . the development of new products and techniques . . .[11]

In determining who solves what problems, assessment must be made as to what is known and what is to be found out: whether it requires a body of theoretical principles, technical knowledge or breakthrough in the state-of-the-art, or an abrupt change in technology, experimentation, or research. Are there gaps in fundamental understanding of the chemical or physical phenomena? If problems fall in this category, they usually must be solved off-line by specialists, engineers, and managers for they require time and appropriate skill and knowledge.

On the other hand, whether the problem requires close and continuous observation of a process, control of a process, or requires hands-on experience and knowledge of small details and local variation; whether there are obvious solutions, which only need to be reduced to practice—these are problems best solved by operators and on-line personnel.

Finally, are the problems departures from well-defined

Passive Observation: Usually On-Line

Studying the Process
Observing Variation

Active Observation: Usually Off-Line

Initiating Changes in the Process
to Discover How to Improve the
Process

SCOPE OF CHANGE

SCOPE	RELATION TO OPERATIONS	HOW IMPROVEMENTS ARE DISCOVERED	TRADITIONAL QC SYSTEM (whose task?)	LABOR-MANAGEMENT QC SYSTEM (whose task?)
New or Improved Product or Process	Off-Line	Research & Technical Analysis Designed Experiments	Engineering and Management	More Time Spent by Engineering & Management
Troubleshoot - Find Cause of Unexpected Change	On-Line & Off-Line	Special Investigations Applied Knowledge	Major Focus for Engineers & Managers Operator (Limited)	Operators & Supervisors with Minimal Help as Needed
Continuous Effort to Optimize the Process	On-Line	Simple Statistical Studies Organized Observation	No One's Focus	More Time Spent by Workers & Supervisors

Table 1-1. Guide for Assessing Quality Improvement Tasks

expectations? Are the causes ambiguous or concealed without obvious answers; do they require investigation or on-line experimentation; do they require both technical knowledge and observation? The advisory committee has authority and resources to conduct experiments, investigations, and obtain technical help It has access to operations and floor experiments and can plan and coordinate these activities. It can establish priorities for departments and have access to information. The advisory committee's role in process improvement is to identify stubborn problems that obstruct quality performance and provide the means to the solution, if not the solution itself. Guiding the improvement task to the proper resource is a key responsibility. Training and skills must be provided to accomplish these tasks.

The process of assignment is self-assignment, not imposed assignment. The Participative Problem Solving® process allows for each constituent group to share in solving the problem based on their knowledge and experience. It would enable each group to reach its highest level of competence, without having to pass the problem on to more technically skilled personnel. The overlapping relationship between the problem-solving teams on the shop floor and the advisory committee allows for input from each level of the problem-solving teams as to who can best work on which problem. Each team, starting at the lowest level, should take over the problem or share of the problems that they can solve.

Many problems that had previously been automatically assigned to staff are now being requested by the problem-solving teams as appropriate problems for them to work on. Staff personnel who are working on problems now have direct access to the machine operators, who have more detailed knowledge of the specific technical problems than the supervisors, who have only a passing knowledge of the technology. This has provided a more effective way of problem assignment. Priorities on these problems are also established by the advisory committee. These priorities determine resource allocation. For example, if support personnel are needed such as maintenance or engineering, design, and technical drawing people, the sequence at which these solutions would be implemented would be determined by the group. And the priorities would be based on importance. In some cases, the problems the teams are working on would receive a higher priority than those the staff people are working on; in some cases, the reverse. Thus, there is no frustration on the part of team members who believe that their problems or solutions have not received support since they are fully cognizant of all of the activities going on in the area and the priorities for each activity. The area manager's job becomes more interesting and more effective, and the union leadership in the area is now recognized for a much broader array of services to both the membership and the company.

The multilevel system creates the environment and structure where fundamental changes to the organization, roles and responsibilities in the quality system can now be contemplated.

A systems diagnosis has now been undertaken by Participative Systems, Inc. with client firms. In this diagnosis, we assess the system in terms of both technical and social criteria. The technical issues are well known but the social issues are not well understood and utilized. Some of the social issues that must be studied are:

- How does the strategic importance of quality affect the social objectives of the organization; for example, wages, benefits, employment security?
- How does the organization of the quality system affect social relations and planning capability in the organization? Does it promote cooperative efforts in contrast to adversarial relationships?
- How well does the quality system advance the scientific and technical skills of all members of the organization?
- How do roles and responsibilities in the quality system affect the psychological health in the organization; for example, worker alienation and management stress?[12]

Some of the results of this diagnosis are as follows:

- The business objectives of quality, as it affects the marketplace, have been well known. Management, in general, and in all functions now are taught that they have quality responsibility; that quality is not only a production or specialist activity. The new development is that labor, both on the shop floor and as union leaders, is now taking the initiative because it sees its relevance to wages, benefits and, most important, employment security.

- The assessment of the quality system in terms of traditional parameters of quality costs and failure rate is too limited. The evaluation must now be made in terms of the rate of quality improvement, as well as the position in the market place in comparison to other domestic and international competitors.

- The traditional quality system is limited by overspecialization, departmentalized engineering and planning and the adversarial relationships that predominate. The multilevel labor-management system directly produces cooperative problem-solving and enhances the planning capability at all levels with the fullest input from management, labor, and the technical support personnel. It also provides the environment where a shift can be organized from a departmentalized focus, where the interest is in the suboptimazation (performance) of each department to a coordinated effort whose concern is the total performance of the whole organization. In some industries, product and process engineering are separated and under different management. Joint teams of engineers and managers can be organized, which will implement a shift from departmentalized engineering to coordinated engineering.

- The principles of suboptimization are seen most keenly in the production process and in traditional organizations which are based on process management. Each individual stage in the process is concerned with the performance of its individual department. Frequently, different products flow through the department with different specifications and requirements, using —without discrimination— the same operators and machines. A shift from process management to product management represents a major opportunity area, particularly for those firms which are producing a variety of products for a number of customers at the same facilities.

- A very important social objective is the advancement of the organization's members in their own skills and educational levels. The labor-management consultative process can and must focus on continued and expanded education and training for all. The quality system depends on the continued growth of scientific and technical knowledge. Training in statistical process control and simple methods of studying, discovering, and designing investigations using statistical methods are now high priority for the multilevel system.

- Self-control for workers and all other employees is a critical shift that is required where control by inspection or supervision is still prevalent. This shift must be planned and organized by the labor-management consultative process so that all benefit by the change. The new roles and responsibilities for workers, inspectors, and foremen can, and must, provide for growth, motivation and security for each person. The labor-management quality system must evaluate these shifts in terms of how it reduces worker alienation and management stess.

- Responsibility for quality must now be expanded to include not only the work that the individual operator or department performs, but also the responsibility to prevent the production of defective products or services. When a defective product is accepted from a prior operation and further work is performed, those who perform such work are violating their responsibility. When a defective product is passed on to subsequent departments, those who pass on that work are violating their responsibility. In summary, the responsibilities include: acceptance of prior work; performance of assigned duties; and quality of the product that is passed on. The execution of this type of responsibility requires an effective direct feedback system. The multilevel consultative process provides the organization with such a system by encouraging direct contact between supervisors and operators in related operations. The principle of timely and direct feedback must also be expanded between different organizations, such as between suppliers and users.

These social objectives produce a motivation and spirit in an organization to obtain a level of quality that cannot be duplicated in a unilateral management system. Quality becomes everybody's business, not only because the company will prosper with high quality, but because each individual member will prosper in terms of those values and those needs felt individually as well as collectively. The labor-management quality system organized through the multilevel organizational structure is an effective, competitive challenge to the total quality control or company-wide quality control system of Japan. The principles of how to organize such a system are now available.

Employment Security

Establishing or increasing employment security requires that we address macro as well as micro issues. Macro issues which can be addressed through national policies will affect the demand for the products and services of various industries. In this regard, import and export policies, as well as interest rates, are among the well-known factors. Industry and labor must continue their efforts to influence macro issues as they relate to employment security. With the advent of international competitive production that can meet any demand, however, the survival and success of any company and plant will depend on the micro issues of productivity and quality. Macro policies will not affect productivity and quality. Increased productivity and quality result from applying human knowledge to improving operations. Knowledge can be used to eliminate waste. The ability to produce greater volume with the same or fewer resources increases productivity. Similarly, knowledge can be used to make products more useful or to reduce defects. Improved productivity and quality increases competitiveness.

Productivity and quality, therefore, must be an operation-by-operation effort, a plant-by-plant effort. This is particularly true because of the international availability of state-of-the-art technology. As quality becomes more important, so does employment security. The application of knowledge at the workplace will only take place when there is security for those who are initiating change. They must have the assurance that this change will not affect their employment security or that of their colleagues. When the development of competence, skills, and knowledge of the workforce continue on an ever-increasing level, the maintenance of this resource is of great importance to the future of the organization.

Therefore, employment security becomes a strategic need for the organization itself, as well as a need for its members. The multilevel system provides the organizational structure to address the micro issue of employment security. The policy committee at the corporate and plant level must develop both short and long-term employment projections; evaluating trends and factors that will affect cyclical dislocations, as well as structural changes in products or process, which in turn will affect production and employment requirements. This committee must evaluate and harmonize structural changes, such as the need for automation, to be competitive and, at the same time, provide strategies to avoid dislocation and unemployment. Automation should be encouraged where it is meaningful, necessary and desirable, but not at the expense of laying off people. A plan is needed to accomplish both objectives.

Alternative plans must be created to develop markets and products, as well as alternative uses of manpower during cyclical downturns. A short-term strategy, which has been tested in Japan since 1973 and tested in a variety of forms on a pilot scale in the United States, provides for alternative plans for utilizing manpower during downturn periods in production requirements. The economic recessions we have experienced in the last 15 years have generally lasted for two years or less. The experience in Japan (1973–1975) indicates that an average 10 percent surplus manpower was maintained in the plants, avoiding layoffs during the recession.

It is my estimate that 10 percent of the manpower in a plant can be utilized effectively to accelerate training and problem-solving which will allow for improvements in productivity and quality. This type of plan, first introduced by the author in testimony to Congress in 1976, and repeatedly raised since then, could be a spur for helping organizations become productive and competitive in quality.[13]

The planning process through the three-tier system, and particularly the middle tier, allows for specific planning on how to utilize people, department by department. It provides for releasing people for accelerated education in problem-solving as well as the development of new skills. It allows for alternative plans that would utilize people productively, thereby justifying maintaining their employment. The cost of their maintenance would be borne by the return on improvements in productivity and quality. A number of companies have already initiated such plans. They have developed systems where surplus personnel could be used to replace others for specialized training or for other activities. Attrition during a recessionary period would normally reduce personnel without a layoff, so having alternative plans in place allows for attrition to take place without replacement. A plan, developing special projects such as the one described in the steel mill, shows the direct return on investment of bringing people off layoff or maintaining them and not allowing them to be laid off in the first place.

Each company that has a joint labor-management process is advised to have a plan in place which will avoid laying people off in the short term. Such an employment maintenance plan would be the principal catalyst for uniting all elements of the organization on a common set of goals and objectives. The employment security, thereby provided with an economic framework that is feasible, would be a highly motivating factor for all parties. This activity could be accelerated further in its implementation if macro policies, like unemployment insurance or supplementary unemployment benefits, were reevaluated so that these funds could be used to maintain people in employment during economic downturns, instead of paying people to be idle. A redirection of those funds to support people in a training environment at the workplace would shift the burden of managing the unemployed from society and from government to that of labor and management leadership at each particular site. They are best qualified to plan for effective use of this manpower. They could also plan for retraining, if the structural requirements would indicate people are needed in different skills and in different jobs.

In the current period of coordinated international production, it is imperative that the principles of productivity and employment security become international in character. For example, Japanese companies with automobile plants in the United States as well as in Japan need to have commitments to job security in both countries. Such practices in one country, and not in another, are destabilizing factors. This is true in many industries. As the commitment to employment security spreads, government, industry, and labor will be motivated to provide more effective planning and policies on a national and international basis.

Leadership in the Next Stage

The nation is still waiting for clear and compelling evidence that a more effective way of organizing and managing our industries has been developed. Significant progress has been made by us and others, yet the process is still in its early stages. The development of the process has been impeded by unrealistic expectations, which caused a warping of our collective judgment as to what is really needed and what we have already achieved. Many projects have been proclaimed as solutions to complex problems when they were only partial systems or hopeful beginnings. Those who make such claims are then hardpressed to defend their current position, when we should all be critically evaluating each project on its merit and pushing on to solve identified problems and develop more advanced systems.

Above all, labor and management leadership is needed now. The multi-tier system as described provides an organizational structure and a set of policies that can allow American industry to change its productivity and quality performance. These principles are now being understood by enlightened trade union leaders and managers. The application of these principles is still very slow, however.

The major barriers are conflicting attitudes within management, within labor, and within the specialist and technical departments. In some mature industries, managers are encouraging joint labor-management cooperation in established organized plants while promoting a union-free environment in new plants. This conflicting behavior precipitates distrust and limits the commitment by both parties.

In some unions, conflicting attitudes prevail among leaders and members. A general recognition exists that current economic and competitive factors require new solutions. Some, however, look to management and government for the solution and reject innovation on the part of labor. They spend their time criticizing union innovators rather than developing strategies that meet the needs of the union as well as the enterprise. These conflicts are frequently fueled by the internal politics of a particular union and do not reflect the commonly accepted necessity for change. This is particularly true in industries where the firms are modest in size. Here, the unions have an especially influential position. The union leaders servicing these plants and firms have an additional responsibility. They must take the initiative to organize and implement the changes needed.

The engineering and technical specialists now are quite aware that they alone cannot solve problems fast enough to be competitive. However, their commitment to professionalism, which promotes exclusivity, has limited the rate at which technical staffs have integrated their work with the joint labor-management process.

Leadership by enlightened managers, labor, and technical personnel is needed to overcome these obstacles. The educational process and theories supporting participative systems must be expanded and used to assist in overcoming these conflicting attitudes.

We can expect the next stage in the development of participative systems to include expanding joint planning and problem-solving to the corporate and international union levels. In recent years, corporate and union policies frequently have not reflected the lessons learned through plant experiences. In some cases, this failure has caused a discontinuity of efforts. The encouraging results that now are being achieved at the plant level will provide the basis by which corporations and international unions can study and evaluate the effect of participative systems on their strategies and policies for the future.

Effective organizations, product quality, and employment security cannot be mandated; they must be created by the affected parties. These goals will be achieved through the initiatives of enlightened and courageous leadership.

REFERENCE NOTES

1. Kaoru Ishikawa, "Quality Control in Japan," Proceedings of the European Organization for Quality Control, February 1979.

2. Irving Bluestone, "Seven Points in the Development of Quality of Worklife Programs," Presented at the Society of Automotive Engineers, International Automotive Engineering Congress and Exposition, March 1977.

3. "Appendix I: Memorandum of Understanding on Labor-Management Participation Teams," *Agreement Between United States Steel Corporation and the United Steelworkers of America*, August 1980, p. 208.

4. "Policy Statement, Edgar Thomson Participative Policy Committee," Joint Policy Statement of US Steel and Local 1219, United Steelworkers of America, August 1980.

5. Thomas C. Graham, Vice Chairman and Chief Operating Officer, US Steel Corporation—Remarks made at the Annual Meeting of the American Iron and Steel Institute Panel on Labor-Management Participation Teams (LMPT), May 1983, pp. 2–3.

6. *Productivity Movement in Japan*, Japan Productivity Center, Tokyo, Japan, January 1981, p.4.

7. Sidney P. Rubinstein, "Quality Control Requires a Social and Technical System;" A Labor Panel, "Labor's Role in Quality," *Quality Progress*, August 1984, p. 27.

8. Henry Mintzberg, *Structure in Fives: Designing Effective Organizations*, Prentice-Hall, Englewood Cliffs, NJ, 1983.

9. Joseph M. Juran, quoted in an interview, "The State of Quality in the U.S. Today," *Quality Progress*, October 1984, p. 37.

10. Rubinstein, *Quality Progress*.

11. Yoshio Kondo, "Company-wide Quality Control in Japanese Industries and Its Impact on Quality of Work Life," Proceedings of QWL and the 1980s, Canadian Council on Working Life, Toronto, Ontario, September 1981.

12. Sidney P. Rubinstein, "Labor-Management Quality Systems Encourage Statistical Process Control," Proceedings of STAQUAREL 1984 Conference, Prague, Czechoslovakia, March 1984.

13. Sidney P. Rubinstein, Oversight Hearings on the Comprehensive Employment and Training Act, House of Representatives, Subcommittee on Manpower, Comprehensive Health and Safety of the Committee on Education and Labor, Washington, DC, September 1976.

Part II

EXPERIENCE

Chapter 2

CASE STUDY: THE INTERLAKE EXPERIENCE

Section 1

OVERVIEW

Gerald J. Shope

Interlake is a Chicago-based corporation with six divisions, primarily in the metals and materials handling businesses. We have approximately $1 billion in sales and approximately 9,000 employees nationwide. I am from the Iron and Steel Division, which is a fully-integrated steel producer. We have two plants in that division with approximately 1,900 employees, providing 25 percent of our corporate sale. Our labor-management participation process is at the Riverdale plant where we produce high or low-carbon strip steel for our various customers. The current employment is approximately 1,200 hourly people at the Riverdale plant location. All our production and maintenance employees are members of the United Steelworkers of America. The hourly work force was organized in 1942.

We began experiencing a significant decline in income and sales in 1974, a situation not uncommon to other steel companies. By 1978, we were in the red. In fact, we were on the verge of a shutdown in early 1982. The reasons were very typical of other steel companies' experience and other heavy industries at that time—increased costs for materials, labor, and energy. At the same time, our productivity had not improved for a number of years. We were adversely affected by foreign competition as well. During 1981 and the early part of 1982, we took some drastic steps to try to save ourselves. There were significant layoffs; we cut spending to the absolute minimum; and we began stretching for efficiencies. Not that we had not been doing some of these things earlier, but we really began to push and stretch. Creativity was considered critical at this point. Another action we took was to ask for union help.

In 1982, we negotiated a new labor agreement. In that agreement, we made a commitment to implement a Labor-Management Participation Team (LMPT) process. The agreement was made in September 1982, and we initiated our LMPT effort in December 1982 with a three-day meeting held off-site. This meeting was attended by all the union and management leadership at the Riverdale location. There were approximately 65 people in attendance. Those present represented all our employees and all our work functions at the Riverdale location. The meeting had two purposes: to provide an orientation in the LMPT process and to identify the needs and concerns of the Riverdale plant. These were expressed in different ways but basically we had a common objective—to save the plant.

So what did we do in this meeting? We agreed to certain goals; we developed a Policy Statement; we adopted a structure; and we developed a strategy. It was a very important three days. The key factor during that three-day period was an expression, a commitment by the labor and management leadership at the plant, to engage in the LMPT process.

We also got to know one another. We discussed common problems and issues. And, please believe me, I don't think there were any issues identified that were in conflict with the overall needs of the plant. Basically, we decided to make this commitment not only to save the plant but also to make the plant a better place to work.

What did we accomplish at the conclusion of these three days? We summarized the needs and concerns that were expressed and put them in writing. We developed our Policy Statement (figure 2-1), which spells out the standards and objectives of our program. We also agreed on a way to implement this process, beginning with orientation meetings throughout the plant for all our employees covering the design and purpose of the LMPT progam. This took three days. After the meetings, we went into the plant and began talking to people one-on-one, as well as in groups, and within a week, we had carried this activity through the entire plant. We provided this orientation so everyone in the plant had an opportunity to become familiar with what was going on. We also selected key people, made a commitment on resources for this process, and decided to establish a group of four coordinator/trainers—two from union, two from management—who would work full-time in the LMPT process. We agreed to start in two divisions and agreed to commit ourselves to training the people who were going to be involved in this process. That commitment included a 40-hour problem-solving training program. We established timetables. I might add that, in establishing our timetables, we were conservative. We targeted initially for seven teams during the first year, and we accomplished that. We had seven viable teams before six months had passed, and we were way ahead of our schedule by the end of the first year. We were conservative. At the time, we didn't have experience in this kind of activity, and we were not too sure of what to expect.

We also agreed on a structure for our LMPT Program. Figure 2-2 describes our structure quite well. The center part of the structure was agreed to, and that particular committee was formed during our three-day, off-site meeting in December 1982. We call that committee the Policy Committee, comprised of 11 members, five from the union and six from the salaried group. Its members are from the union leadership and plant management. The group includes among others, the union president and vice president, plant manager, two general superintendents, and the manager of employee relations. The policy committee group has, as its primary responsibility, ensuring that the proper environment exists for the LMPT process. In the beginning, our efforts were concentrated and focused on implementation and what our strategy would be. We concerned ourselves with carrying out those particular objectives.

The policy committee meets monthly. There is also a subcommittee, including the plant manager and the union president, that meets weekly for an update on LMPT activities provided by the coordinator/trainers.

POLICY STATEMENT

RIVERDALE PLANT LMPT POLICY COMMITTEE

Described in Appendix H of the 1980 Labor Agreement and reconfirmed by both Union and Management in the 1982 Labor Agreement, Labor-Management Participation Teams (LMPT) is a system in which employees, both hourly and salaried, have the opportunity to work together; not just in their traditional roles, but on problem solving teams in a joint effort to solve the serious problems which face all employees at the Riverdale Plant both today and in the future. Participation Teams will be open on a voluntary basis to all members of United Steelworkers of America, Local 1053 and all salaried employees at the Riverdale Plant. Participation Teams will be gradually expanded on a departmental and divisional basis to ensure the success of this effort in an orderly and realistic manner.

Participation Teams will attempt to identify and solve serious problems of mutual interest that affect all employees at the Riverdale Plant with the objective of:

- Enhancing job security and earnings for all employees - hourly and salaried - by producing a top quality, competitive product and delivering it on time
- Improving the safety of the work place
- Reducing production costs and improving efficiency by working smarter
- Encouraging each employee to express his or her ideas and thus have more input in decisions that are made
- Improving and strengthening the relationship between hourly employees and salaried employees
- Providing an atmosphere which promotes dignity and pride in workmanship for all employees

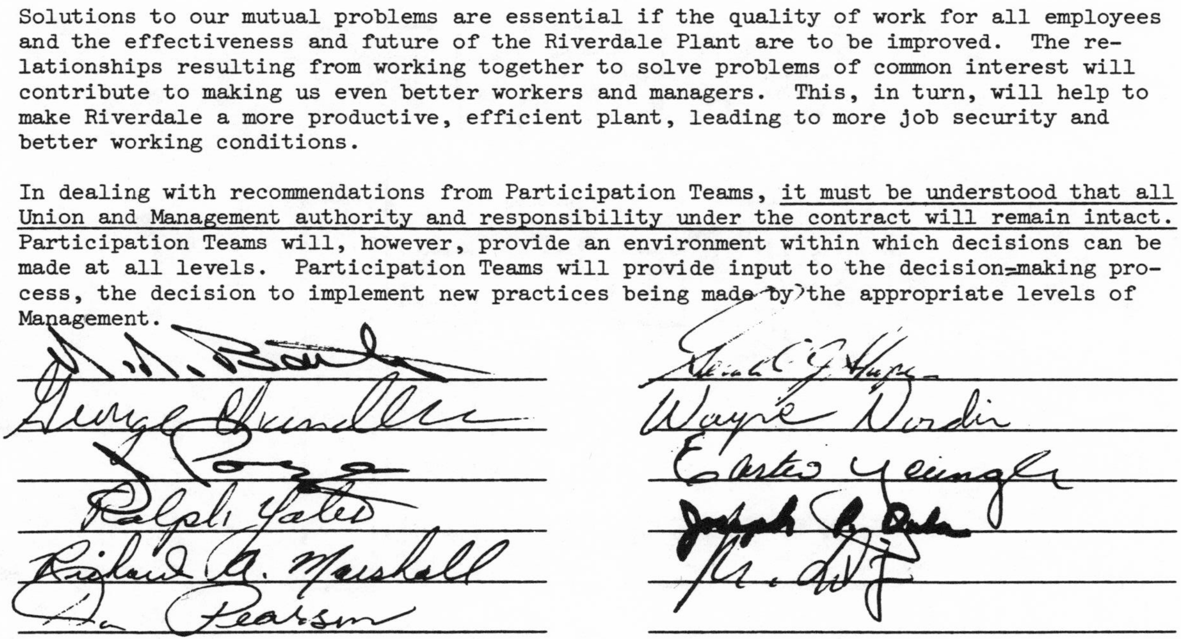

Solutions to our mutual problems are essential if the quality of work for all employees and the effectiveness and future of the Riverdale Plant are to be improved. The relationships resulting from working together to solve problems of common interest will contribute to making us even better workers and managers. This, in turn, will help to make Riverdale a more productive, efficient plant, leading to more job security and better working conditions.

In dealing with recommendations from Participation Teams, it must be understood that all Union and Management authority and responsibility under the contract will remain intact. Participation Teams will, however, provide an environment within which decisions can be made at all levels. Participation Teams will provide input to the decision-making process, the decision to implement new practices being made by the appropriate levels of Management.

Figure 2-1. Policy Statement—Riverdale plant LMPT policy committee.

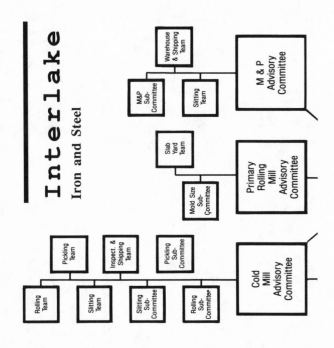

Figure 2-2.   Structure of Interlake, Inc.

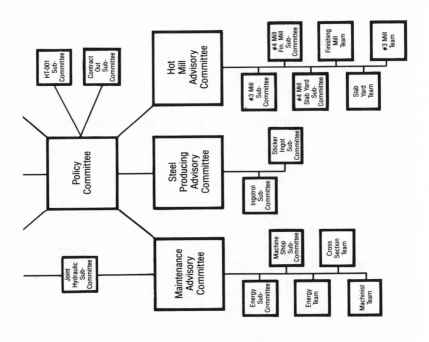

Today, we are beginning to focus on more long-range planning issues, although we still concern ourselves with maintenance and some administrative activities that need to be attended to.

The next level in this three-tiered structure are the advisory committees. These committees represent our operating divisions and maintenance division. Right now, all of our operating and maintenance areas are included in the LMPT process. The advisory committee consists of the division superintendent, his general foreman, the union leadership in that particular division, and, often, some hourly personnel who are members of the union but not necessarily union officials. We have some staff people on those committees as well. In the beginning, their efforts were to support the team process in their respective divisions. They went through 32 hours of problem-solving training, so in addition to being an administrative group, they are also a problem-solving group. The advisory committees, meeting weekly, have been active in problem-solving activities from the beginning. In fact, some of the advisory committees have broken into subcommittees to work on a variety of problems. Some of the advisory committees from different divisions have come together to work on specific problems. For example, we have had maintenance and cold mill groups that formed a team to work on common problems.

I'll be frank. In the beginning, when I looked at this organizational structure, I thought it was going to be perhaps a little bit heavy on bureaucracy. It has turned out to be an ideal arrangement in our situation, however, because it has provided our middle management—our general foreman in particular—a role in the LMPT process. And we're seeing significant accomplishments as a result of the advisory committee's problem-solving activities. They are a key support—a very important part of this whole process.

Then, of course the teams—they are in all our operating and maintenance areas, usually eight to nine members per team. Usually, a foreman is included in the team process. In the beginning, it was a bit difficult to get foremen to join teams, not so much because they were against the process, but we have been running lean, and this was another responsibility we were putting on our front-line supervisors. As time went by, we had more participation by these supervisors, and I believe now the membership of most of our teams includes a foreman. Technical and staff personnel will supply support to any of these three levels— the policy committee, the advisory committees, and to the teams themselves. By technical staff support, I am describing industrial engineering, metallurgy, plant engineering, accounting, purchasing, etc., whatever the need may be.

The consultative intermediary was Participative Systems, Inc. (PSI). PSI in our situation is very important. They were with us from the beginning. Today, we are able to function more independently, but, PSI is still with us. We're two years into the process, and they are still an important part of the effort.

To everyone in the process, we provided information about quality problems, product and material costs; information that had never been made available. As an example, we provided a good deal of information about energy costs. As a steel producer, energy costs are a significant item to us. We provided unit costs, as well as conversion costs in our products and materials. This kind of information was useful in helping our teams select problems and helping them to identify where the problems were—not that anyone dictated to the team what they had to do or what kinds of problems they had to work on. As a result, when everyone had the same information, they were able to identify priorities more effectively.

At this point, we have 34 operating teams. We have approximately 55 completed projects out of the 133 that were undertaken. The net savings today are approximately $750,000. There still are some difficulties, but these problems are not as significant to us as they were in the beginning. Skepticism is certainly still there; not everyone is enthusiastic; not everyone has become involved. With respect to the general foremen and middle managers, however, we've seen an improvement. In the beginning, the general foremen were asked to participate in the advisory committes, and in most cases, they did. But, quite frankly, they will tell you now that in the beginning they didn't want to. They did not want any part of it. Their superintendent asked them to participate and they felt they couldn't say "no". Today, these same general foremen will tell you, "I'm glad I'm in it. I'm glad I'm here and I don't want out!" Not all of them, of course, but a good number of them will. Supervisory participation has improved.

Project implementation frustration was probably one of the more significant problems we experienced in the process. The hourly teams began to complain that, after they've gone through problem selection, problem solution, and obtaining authorization to implement the problem solution, the implementation involved maintenance skills and manhours which weren't always available. For example, teams were saying, "I don't see my project. Where is it? We've waited months." We had not instituted a good tracking system, so we played catch-up. We did find many of the projects were being implemented. The people who were complaining, however, were those who weren't seeing their solutions implemented. Once we gave them feedback, however, they were satisfied. We now have the ability to supply feedback through a tracking system. It did not require us to provide a new system. We found out we had the ability within our existing system to track, so another bureaucracy was not created.

Recently, we had a group of visiting businessmen from England who were part of the Industrial Participation Association. A few of them raised questions regarding the cost justification aspect of our system. We do require teams to cost justify their problem solutions. In responding to these questions, we explained we were not doing cost justifications to keep score or to defend the process, but that these teams are competing for capital monies, for expense budgets, for resources, manpower, whatever it might be. They are competing within the system. We haven't created a separate system, so they have to cost justify. That is the only way they are going to get attention. In our system it's very crucial, and it's working. Probably the group you have to watch is the advisory committee because there you have the superintendent and the general foremen and they have the power to implement. But the teams are certainly using cost justification procedures, and we expect the advisory committees to do the same.

Sometimes the head manager dominated. In the beginning, we believed that perhaps this was an example of the typical autocratic style of management in some of our operations. It wasn't, however. We found that the hourly people were a bit reluctant and a bit inhibited. The superintendent was naturally taking over to try to maintain the process. Through the coordinator/trainers and some other efforts, including some training, we were able to get the hourly participants, especially within the advisory committees, to be more participative. In fact, the superintendents were relieved to see that happen; it let them off the hook. They really didn't want to dominate the process. So there's been improvement there.

Insufficient meeting time is always going to be a problem, especially in a continuous operation such as we have. We are rotating turns, which adds additional complications. We realize people aren't always able to attend meetings, and so we have to contend with this problem.

Poor meeting rooms are problems but we have done a lot there. If you survey your plant many times, you will find there are meeting rooms you didn't know existed.

Right now the future as we see it, espcially from the policy committee's perspective, includes expansion of the LMPT process. For the remainder of the year, however, we have taken the position that we would like to stay at our present level, monitor the process to ensure that it is healthy, and next year begin to increase the number of teams. We expect the advisory committees to determine the number of teams and designate the areas, whereas in the beginning this was done by the policy committee. This activity will be more in the advisory committee's hands from now on.

Increased training, awareness, and competence—this is an ongoing process. We have continued to carry on these activities with our coordinator/trainers and with the team leaders. These activities will always be part of the process. To provide more depth to the program, we are starting to link some of our future needs at the Riverdale plant into the LMPT process. We just recently had the plant manager share detailed information about our five-year strategic plan with the policy committee. This was subsequently done with one of the divisions, and we are going to continue to do this throughout the LMPT process. We want to make people aware of changing expectations, new technologies, market trends, and what our manpower and training needs are going to be. We believe the LMPT process will be able to complement our efforts to achieve future objectives. We can coordinate information and ideas from the top of the organization all the way down to the shop floor so we can all share the same objectives. To give an example, we have recently seen a trend in our business to higher carbon specialty steels. That has implications for our operations—our quality—and we have already seen some teams tackle problems that are going to help us move into these markets more successfully. In the area of manpower training, we are currently providing job skill improvement training for our craft employees. Most of this training is being provided by local colleges. Our people are going to school on their own and, at this point, are showing a good deal of enthusiasm. It is working out well. We are also expecting to be able to mesh the LMPT system process with our existing quality system and the use of process control techniques. We certainly see this happening in the very near future.

I believe that summarizes the particulars. Now, some comments about the benefits. I believe we have seen just the beginning of them. I can not document the change in morale, which has improved, but I can certainly document performance improvement. We had to operate at between 90 and 95 percent capacity in 1982 to break even. We are now able to break even at approximately 75 percent capacity and even make some modest profit this year. Then there is the issue of security. Job security is certainly something we all want to maintain. We want to save our jobs as well as save the plant. "For our future"—that is our logo. I might add, this is a belief we have adhered to very faithfully, and I believe the logo symbolizes that. From the beginning in summer 1982, both union and management participants throughout the LMPT program structure have not made decisions independently of each other. Union members and officials are involved throughout the process—they are involved from the policy committee to the shop floor. When we have delicate problems, and they do exist, and they will exist in the future, we have an understanding of what this process is about and what some of the requirements for working with it are. We have been very careful, I think successfully so in that respect, to keep non-LMPT matters out of the LMPT process. We still have grievances. We still have various committees that have their foundations in the Labor Agreement and business goes on as normal in those areas. I believe we now have the ability to communicate, and at least try, to convey our understandings a little more successfully than we did a few years ago, but we have been very careful to restrict grievances from flowing into this process because this would be very damaging.

This has been a quick overview of our experience and, though it may sound simplistic, this is what we have done, and it has worked.

Section 2

LABOR'S PERSPECTIVE

Don Pearson

The United Steelworkers Local 1053 is involved in LMPT for a variety of reasons. We believe that the single most important reason is the job. We agree with Sid Rubinstein that job security is a real issue. Our union has already provided something that Sam Camens referred to before—earnings security, but at Local 1053 we feel it is not enough.

Membership in our union has been drastically affected in the last few years. Local 1053 represented approximately 1,800 workers in 1970. Today that figure is slightly more than 1,100. In the last two years, however, we were down under 1,000. United Steelworkers of America (USWA) District 31 covers the entire Calumet region in Illinois and Indiana. Our membership was once 120,000. Today it is approximately 70,000. Our International union was once 1.4 million strong; today it is approximately 750,000. These declines in membership have been contributed to by a variety of reasons: imports, poor management, high labor costs, high energy costs, among others. In Local 1053, we believe a major portion is because of a lack of in-depth participation. Participation not only through the suggestion box system that we've always had, but in the real decision-making process which will help Riverdale remain viable. When we do that we will be protecting the jobs of our members.

Since 1959, the year of the last strike at our plant, relations between Interlake and Local 1053 have been what you might call amicable. We have had isolated battles both in negotiations and the grievance procedure but no long-running feud between management and the union. Workers in our plant experienced some slow times, but they were always short-term. They could always say, "Well, I'm laid off but I'm going to go back." We always had definite time periods that we were able to stabilize.

In the 1970s profits began to decline in Riverdale. Membership began to decline and the future of somebody retiring with 30 years of service became questionable in people's minds. Negotiations began to take on a different note and became so tense, in 1980, that agreement was reached only after a one-week extension. At that time, however, the economy continued to devastate our membership and, in 1982, Interlake approached our union with a proposal to renegotiate an agreement that was less than two years old. At first, the union said 'okay', but we didn't mean it. We didn't agree that we had to negotiate. Management stated that the plant was in danger of closing, and when the union asked about profits and costs at Interlake the company produced their books and gave them to our international union. I believe that this one act of producing the books and giving them to our International so they could look at them helped a great deal in producing the environment that created LMPT. Before, we never heard of anything like that. Well, our auditors went over the books and came back and told us that Interlake was not lying; they were telling the truth that the plant was in grave danger of closing.

So we entered into negotiations. We negotiated an agreement, and although this agreement included concessions of approximately $1.35 an hour, it also included a commitment that Interlake and Local 1053 would join together in LMPT. I do not know if everybody knows that in 1980 we had an experimental LMPT agreement that was never implemented for a variety of reasons. Neither the union nor the company was willing to say, "Okay, we're going to do this." Historically, union officials have always been reactors. They wait for the company to make a decision and then they act accordingly. At Local 1053, we feel that although reaction is still a part of our duty and a part of our job because we have to protect our membership, it is not enough. We must become involved in those decisions before they are made. We must be a part of those decisions because, after all, our jobs and the future of our families are at stake. Our members, as workers in the plant, know their jobs. They know where improvement can be made. They now have the opportunity to have some input. We have a responsibility to those members— the responsibility of helping to provide that job security.

We have union people involved in all three levels of our structure. Hourly workers comprise the majority of team membership and many have even assumed the role of leaders. Grievance committeemen are involved on just about all the advisory committees, and on the policy committee are four executive board members and one grievance man. The policy committee decided the overall implementation plan for LMPT. We outlined a pay structure and discussed problems from both sides.

The union also sees itself finally being included in the process of the plant. For many years, members and union officials have wanted to be included—we are always told that it is management's job—they'll run the plant. We believe that the surest way to provide job security for our members is through modernization. We believe, however, that we must take an active part in that modernization. We not only need to know what's going to happen—where our plant is going, but also how modernization and advancing technology is going to have an affect on jobs. We need and we are creating a committee that looks at jobs. We just recently constructed a list of all our maintenance people in crafts in an effort to project how many of those people are going to be leaving and to project if there is any additional training they need. Our union does not want to see people retire, or quit, and then have the company go out and hire somebody else. The union also sees as its role that of being a third party—someone that is bridging the gap between hourly and salaried personnel. I did not believe that was always the case. When we first started, I wasn't sure if I could sit down with management and work on something, but you have to have the union involved. The union can also help bridge the gap that has been created in plants between different levels and different functions of management. We found out through joint committees that it is often the union people that bring production and maintenance together or one division with another. Divisions in our plants can no longer just do their parts and say, "I did mine and here it is" to the next division or "you do what you can do with this." We also believe that managers should not be judged only on production levels, but in how the hourly workers respond and whether those same workers are allowed input.

Another role for the union is to assure that the giant strides made in the past are not lost. We need to tear down barriers but we must protect our members' rights and benefits as we have in the past. As mentioned earlier, union officials have always been reactors. We react to items such as discipline, contracting out, and job combination and elimination. But at Local 1053 we have taken it on as an extra duty to become part of those decisions before they are made. This way, we feel we can better represent our workers and the transition period can become smoother. Reacting is just not good enough any longer.

A third thing we see as our role is that of communicator. For many long-standing reasons, hourly personnel will just not respond when a manager walks up to them and says, "I want you to get involved." They're more apt to listen. We believe that by having union officials who are elected representatives of the members, the communications will flow better. Hourly personnel have seen many company programs come in and go out and it has been the same old thing. Now they see their union and management joining together in a cooperative effort to improve for the better of all.

Section 3

TRAINING

Ralph Yates

When we began, we started training advisory committees first. That was middle management and divisional union leadership-superintendents, assistant superintendents, general foremen, engineers, metallurgists, grievance committeemen, and some of our executive board. Where have you ever seen grievance committeemen and superintendents sitting down together talking about common problems? It was a first for me, and it really worked out. I did not believe at first it was going to work. I have to be truthful because I was a grievance man for 20 years, and there were a couple of superintendents I did not get along with, but it's working. It worked out beautifully. They received 32 hours of training and it was very intense. We really relied more on PSI for that training.

Participation in LMPT is voluntary. The four coordinator trainers conduct the 40-hour Participative Problem Solving® training course for teams. We had three weeks of training by PSI here at Princeton to prepare us for this role.

The subjects of our training course include the history and background of labor-management in the United States, team-building exercises, leadership, and trust. We also cover problem-solving tools. We show them the problem-solving sequence, problem identification, and problem selection criteria. Data analysis, statistical process control, and a number of problem-solving strategies are also included. We also teach the teams to implement solutions, test them and evaluate the results.

In addition to the training for the policy committee, advisory committees, and coordinator trainers, PSI has given us some other special training. Saul Rubinstein has also come out to train union leaders. We don't say the company should buy it, but the union does have to buy it. And, if you are not sincere when you go in there, you just don't get involved. I am directing this to union leaders right now. Management has to go through the same thing, but people in the union must be sincere. They really do. They have to believe in it, and give it a chance.

At first, I was a little skeptical. After I became a coordinator/trainer, the first question I asked was how much do we pay outside contractors for servicing our air conditioning. I have been in six negotiations and always have asked and was always told it was none of my damned business. It wasn't any of my business. As soon as LMPT went into effect, I went and asked them, and they gave me the book and said, "Here it is." I couldn't believe it, and they have done this with every team out there. Anything that they have asked for they have received. They have yet to be refused. That is how much management and staff have helped us.

Other than the union officials being trained, we had some special training on quality. Sid Rubinstein and Bob Loekle came out to help train our division heads and some top union officials in quality systems and the use of statistics.

We also had some help with team leaders. These teams meet once a week, usually for an hour—they must have a team leader. The team leader didn't really know what he was supposed to do, and I didn't know what the team leader was supposed to do either, to be truthful. We tried to help them out. We tried to keep the meetings going, but through PSI and their assistance, we got all the team leaders together. And now, periodically, we have team leaders training and meetings for them so they can share each other's views. It has been very helpful for team leaders to hear about the problems other team leaders have in different areas of the plant, and how they got around their problems. That has helped out.

Now, I shall go to the last part. We also conducted an LMPT exhibition. We had a tent outside on company property—a 100 x 40 foot tent—and we asked the teams, if they wanted— strictly voluntary again—to put up the displays of what they had worked on, what they had done. We had people out there for two days, 12 hours a day, explaining what their exhibits were. We had a great response.

Section 4

STRATEGIC PLANNING

Saul A. Rubinstein

When we evaluate a joint Labor-Management Problem-Solving System, we look at the results it has produced, as well as the principles and values underlying its design. We also try to project its tendencies toward stability and continuity.

For the participation effort to be sustained, it must be both effective and efficient. By effective we mean it must solve the right problems, those which are closely and consistently linked to operational priorities. These priorities, in turn, must be addressed through the involvement of the entire work force. For Interlake or any organization to be most efficient, it must use all of its resources, particularly its human resources. The organization must be in a position to solve critical problems through joint labor-management participation in problem-solving. Only in this way will a system make both operational and organizational sense.

In creating a stable, long-lasting, effective participation process, several elements are essential. These include:

- A **culture** or **environment** which supports the partici-pative system. Organizational values and conditions must encourage increased workforce involvement in problem-solving and decision-making. Relationships between labor and management must change from adversarial to cooperative in areas where a common interest can be identified.

- A **strategic planning** approach to problem selection. The organization must develop a systematic way for priority problems and opportunities to be jointly identified and addressed by labor-management problem-solving groups.

- An organizational **structure** which will:

  1. support joint labor-management problem-solving groups at all levels of the organization;

  2. provide for all functional areas to participate in problem-solving activities as well as interact with each other in a nonadversarial way. This applies not only to labor-management relationships, but also to the relationships within management; for example, quality and production, production and maintenance, engineering and operations, one manufacturing department to another, etc.

     Furthermore, in a multiunion setting, the structure must provide for the interaction of the various labor organizations in a way which supports the values and goals of the participative process in the organization as a whole.

- Training in new **skills.** It is not sufficient to simply create an appropriate organizational environment or culture, develop a strategy to establish direction, and create a structure and organization to support problem-solving involving all levels and functions. Participation requires that people relate to one another in new ways, identifying and solving problems as groups. This necessitates training in the skills necessary to help people function successfully in these new roles.

- Effective **leadership** from labor and management. Both the implementation and long term continuity of these systems require leadership at all levels: plant policy committee, divisional advisory committees, departmental subcommittees, and shop-floor teams. At each level, leadership must come from both labor and management.

I will leave the issues of environment, structure, skills, and leadership to the other authors and focus on the issue of strategic planning.

Strategic planning in a Participative Problem Solving® process has as its objectives:

   I.   Establishing priorities for problem-solving.
  II.   Planning improvement projects.
 III.   Managing resource allocation.

These three objectives lead to the fourth.

 IV.   Increasing the rate of quality and productivity improvement. (This determines competitiveness in the world market.)

Many people raise questions as to how problems get selected, and how we know whether the right problems are being solved. Strategic planning in the participative system starts with an effort to identify the most critical problems and challenges that the organization faces, so that they can be addressed through the labor-management problem solving process. One of the key issues, therefore, is problem selection. In any organization we must have a process to identify the priority problems that need to be solved to meet the common objectives of both labor and management.

The basic strategy is to:

1. Identify the future <u>direction</u> of the organization. This requires an analysis of the business including strengths, weaknesses, future opportunities, competitive position, and market niche. It also includes an examination of the organi-

zation's stated goals and objectives. The following detailed information is necessary:

A. Changes in product mix;
B. New product introductions;
C. Quality problems and requirements;
D. Production costs;
E. Capital plans for new equipment and new technology.
F. Manpower and skill requirements.

2. Identify the problems, challenges and priorities associated with that direction.

3. Identify those problems which can be addressed through the Labor-Management Problem-Solving System.

4. Determine the most appropriate level (plant policy committee, divisional advisory committee, departmental subcommittee, shop-floor team) in the system to solve the problem. This ensures the most efficient use of all resources.

Each level in the Participative Problem Solving® System has a unique role to play in this planning process (described in Figure 2-3). The **policy committee** is the most appropriate group to establish the overall organizational **goals** or **themes** for problem solving. The divisional **advisory committees** can then determine more specific **objectives** consistent with the themes, and feed this back to the policy committee. The **teams** identify **problems** based on their knowledge of the operation and input from their advisory committee on the department's peformance, priority problems, targets and challenges for the coming year.

In larger organizations, planned improvement projects are coordinated through departmental **subcommittees** of the advisory committee working closely with **teams.** Jointly, they establish priorities and targets, coordinate the problem-solving effort, and allocate resources. This is illustrated in Figure 2-4.

For example, when Interlake decided to shift its product mix toward more high carbon and specialty steels, some of the teams decided to take a look at some of the manufacturing problems associated with those products. One of the teams developed a new approach to slitting high carbon material. They slit the steel while it is still hot, rather than allowing it to cool. As a

Figure 2-3.   Strategic planning in the LMPT system.

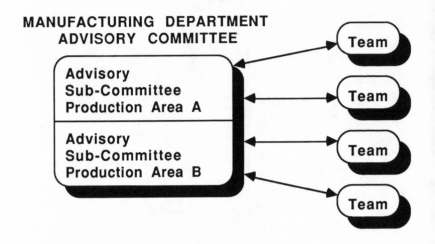

Figure 2-4. Team and advisory committee coordination of planned improvement projects.

result they obtain a better quality slit edge with less wear on the cutting tools.

This type of planning activity requires a great deal of information sharing. In addition to information on manufacturing costs, yield, raw materials and quality, information from the customer is essential. For example, the customer can provide critical input on quality needs, end use changes, specifications, volume shifts, packaging and delivery leading to more effective problem selection.

Some of the Interlake teams have analyzed customer complaints, and a special problem-solving team has been set up jointly with one customer to focus on edge defects. Customer complaints and internal scrap and repair data will help the teams identify the most critical current problems. But, it is important to involve marketing as well, because marketing determines the organization's future direction in terms of products and services. This information includes how the competitive profile is changing, and which market niche the organization can be most successful in pursuing.

If we are not successful in linking strategy in problem selection to our system of participation in problem-solving, then over time its direction and the direction of the company will diverge. If this occurs, the problem-solving system will fade away, getting less attention since it is not focused on the organization's most significant challenges. The only way to keep Labor-Management Participation Teams and the direction of an organization on the same path is through a process of long-term and strategic planning within the LMPT system, setting its direction.

In summary, strategic planning is important for the following reasons: first, to make sure that we are identifying and addressing the key problems; second, to ensure the long term stability of the participation system.

Creating a system to solve problems requires an investment in resources. Introducing an approach of strategic planning in problem selection to a Labor-Management Participation Team system ensures that these resources are used in a meaningful way.

Chapter 3

THE ETHICON ACHIEVEMENT

Clark Leslie

I have been in manufacturing and operations for 30 years with Procter & Gamble and then with Johnson & Johnson, of which Ethicon is a part. I have 17 or 18 years' experience working with the Amalgamated Clothing & Textile Workers Union (ACTWU) and 10 years working in the area of work involvement and participation. The dream of high productivity, high commitment, and high job satisfaction seems like a lifelong quest. Many of the early efforts really were aimed at trying to get management's act together, trying to get management to talk to each other, and trying to get management to communicate. You probably remember sensitivity training, the managerial grid and the many OD programs of the 1960s and 1970s. There also were many scattered and fragmented efforts to include the workers in participative efforts. We were encouraged by the reports of the behavioral scientists. We were encouraged by reports of the dog food plant in Topeka and the many other experiments around the country that were being reported, most of them in brand new plants where the culture was built from the ground up. There were always many questions as to whether the kind of environment necessary for participation could be developed in a traditional plant with a long history of a different kind of environment.

Within Johnson & Johnson at the Eastern Surgical Dressing Plant (ESDP), which is also represented by ACTWU Local 630, a number of small efforts were begun, in individual departments, to include the workers in the decision-making processes for those departments. Most of them died as managers changed, as the situation changed or as processes changed. Initially, the union was not involved. The union did not oppose. The union observed. Top management also was not involved. These were local experiments, many of them very successful during the short time that they lived.

About seven years ago, two breakthroughs occurred that I believe are really the foundations upon which our effort at Ethicon is based. One began when we had an outside audit of our incentive systems. Those who have worked with incentive systems over a long period of time know what happens as they lose their viability, as they become watered down by various agreements or changes in the pay structure. The consultant who audited the incentive system reported back to us what we all knew—nobody liked the incentive system: management did not; the workers did not; nobody claimed ownership. It was just there, and it was more a hindrance than a help to what we were trying to do.

The incentive systems were part of our labor contract. Management has a right to eliminate the incentive systems but we could not unilaterally change them. So really, the only way to change them was to sit down with the union (and the workers) and work together on a change. Right away management was faced with a cultural question and that was whether we should tell the union what the consultants said; tell the union how bad things really were. Should we give them the whole report or just select pages of the report?

We decided that we had to bring them in as full partners and gave them the whole report. Obviously, there were no surprises in the report; they knew the situation as well as anybody. We began the joint effort at that time—a steering committee of top management and top union officials working down through individual incentive task forces in the individual departments of the plant. It was a long, slow process, and we went through the confidence-building and trust-building that is so necessary after a long history of an adversarial relationship. That process is still ongoing at ESDP, and that experience with Local 630 and Johnson & Johnson management showed that we could work together in a cooperative way.

At almost the same time, the management at ESDP set up a seminar on participation and invited management from other J & J facilities and outside experts. We had the plant manager from the Topeka Dog Food plant. We had other outside experts and consultants, including one who had apparently done some interesting things at the Tarrytown General Motors plant. That meeting occurred here at the Chauncey Conference Center and was when I first met Sid Rubinstein. Sid brought something to this deal that others did not, and that was a clear understanding of the role of the worker and the union in productivity and quality improvement.

Shortly afterwards, we began at ESDP joint union-management work involvement efforts, training seminars, a steering committee, developed a charter and, ultimately, an agreement that layoffs would not result from participation in the participative program.

These two experiences formed the foundation for both management, Local 630 and Sid Rubinstein to begin developing a joint effort at Ethicon. In my experience, what we did in the 1960s and 1970s was really done on faith, the gut feeling that we could do better if everyone participated. At Johnson & Johnson at that time, we certainly were not being pressed by foreign competition or by the marketplace. We were just doing our job and trying to do it better.

It was five years ago when I came to Ethicon, a company that certainly had no reason to be concerned about the future— a market share in the high 70s and the highest quality reputation in the business. We were very profitable and the price leader, so costs were not a problem. Because of our size and our significant vertical integration for our industry, we were probably also the low-cost manufacturer. The company was marketing and finance-oriented, had labor intensive processes, and a fair relationship with our wage force and with the union.

It also was obvious that there was much opportunity for improvement. Our first effort was to provide manufacturing with a tool for understanding their operations and improving productivity, and we brought in a consultant to install a semi-traditional, short-interval scheduling process. We conceived that this might also be the basis for a work involvement effort; that the problems turned up by the close observation of the processes that evolved through the short-interval scheduling technique would lead to the identification of problems that could be solved by teams of wage employees. So we concurrently attempted to start up a participative system. We established a steering committee and wrote a charter.

We found that in the people's and union's mind, the short-interval scheduling effort, which was seen as a management tool for making people work harder and faster, was inconsistent with a joint effort to work smarter. Because of that dichotomy in our first approach, the effort lay dormant for some time.

We tried later, by bringing in Sid, whom the union already knew from their experience at ESDP, and we started again. We, again, had to face the problems of trust and confidence. Management certainly had to change their approach. The idea of participation at Ethicon was a new idea. It took some management rotation to develop the atmosphere that finally made the program work.

As we became involved, we, in management, had to face up to the issue of job security. It was an issue that had been a subject of management concern independently of the work involvement effort, but certainly the work involvement effort brought it to a head for us. Historically, the Somerville, New Jersey plant had suffered wide fluctuations in job levels. A 10 percent change in employment level was not at all unusual from year-to-year: lots of layoffs, lots of rehiring with high training costs resulting from the bumping and bidding processes as we went up and down in manpower. Our practice had been to level load our other facilities and take the fluctuations at Somerville. The wisdom of that decision really had never been challenged. It was an economically poor decision and, certainly from a relationship standpoint, it was a poor decision.

We decided that we would try and manage our business

without layoffs in all four, and now five, of our manufacturing locations. We did it because we believe we had an obligation to our loyal employees, and it became apparent that it was good business to avoid the inefficiencies of the bumping, hiring, bidding, and retraining. So we were able to enter into an understanding with the union that we would try to avoid layoffs. We could not guarantee that we would avoid layoffs.

J & J has a credo that says, 'our people shall be secure in their jobs,' and we certainly have taken that into our consideration. In the past, that was interpreted to mean that, if the company succeeds and grows, we are all more secure in our jobs, and the thought process really had not moved much beyond that. Our efforts over the last three or four years, I believe, have been very evident, very successful, and, certainly, very sincere in avoiding layoffs. It has meant balancing production between our five plants and adjusting manning on the basis of attrition, when necessary, to reduce head count.

I believe it has been of great benefit to Ethicon to operate in that manner. The union has cooperated in this effort in working with us to operate with increased flexibility and make necessary adjustments to facilitate keeping the people employed. This has been a real breakthrough at Ethicon. Not all management has supported it, however. When we first became involved at Ethicon, those who were involved certainly had a reasonable fear that maybe this was a passing fad and that as management changed, they might be stuck with a program that lacked top management support. The program is working well, however. We are training volunteers; problem solving is occurring; incentive task forces are working; there is an increased level of communication and cooperation between the union and management; and, we have effectively avoided layoffs. We have carried some excess people, and now we are making our first attempt at using some of those excess people in problem-solving. Many problems remain on both the management and union side.

The environment for our project changed significantly two years ago. The health care business caught up with the rest of the world as a result of the government changing the way they funded Medicare. For the first time in many years, the health care industry came under cost and price pressure. Our market share declined; our competitor's quality improved, and we face new competitors. We are under heavy price competition. We are facing major inventory reductions by all of the hospitals and the dealers, and facing very tough competition now on product features and quality.

What started out in Somerville as a nice thing to do and something that seemed right is now getting closer to being a matter of survival. Somerville, because of its location in the northeast, is our high-cost plant. Our major competitor has their largest operation in Puerto Rico. The first trickle of Japanese products is beginning to appear in this country. The number one objective of Ethicon at this time is cost reduction. We are committed to maintaining Somerville as a viable manufacturing operation. We are shifting products between plants so that the least labor-intensive products will be produced in Somerville and, although we have moved products out of Somerville to our other plants, we have brought products back to Somerville that fit this new strategy. Our most highly automated processes will be installed in Somerville. Developmental processes that require the support of the central engineering and central research staffs will also be operated in Somerville.

Those are the kinds of processes that are going to work best with the full involvement of all of the employees and the union. Participation is the key part of our strategy now to keep the Somerville plant competitive. The union is working with us to accomplish that, and we are committed to achieving this change in role for the plant without layoffs, using only attrition when head-count reduction is required. The problem-solving teams and the worker commitment are leading to the highest productivity ever experienced in those departments where we have the longest participative experience.

What are the management problems in this environment? What are my problems within this environment? With the new cost pressure, I am questioning our strategy: why not close Somerville down? Why not downsize it faster? Is the no-layoff policy really paying off? Are not we penalizing ourselves with a no-layoff policy? Fortunately, we started when we did, and we have been successful enough and have enough solid results not only to defend our position and strategy for Somerville, but enthusiastically to endorse it and win the support of the management board.

Recently, we have begun the introduction of a quality program, which we are trying to fit into the work involvement participative effort. I believe it is a good step, but we are running into problems of semantics, and trust; how does it fit, what are the definitions, what are the requirements—just one more complication in the long story of our effort.

Top management at J & J is very traditional. It is okay to try new things if it works. Again, we have been successful, and I believe we are providing a model for all of J & J. I believe the union leadership has similar problems. I know that the union leadership is committed to making this process work, but I believe they have the same kind of top management problems, skepticism and traditional views that we have. We also jointly have the complexity, interjected by Ethicon's nonunion plants in the southeast and southwest. The textile workers tried unsuccessfully to organize one of our plants, which certainly led to much stress and strain on this program. The strength of the program, I believe, is proven by the fact, under that type of situation, both union and management kept this program going.

There are likely to be many more such complications as our business becomes increasingly cost competitive, and we must look for other ways to reduce costs. There is always the possibility of off-shore sourcing, particularly as we watch our competition head in that direction. I believe the challenge that Sid has defined so well in the past is to prove that the plant in the northeast with a union working cooperatively with management, and with management recognizing the needs of the union and the people, particularly in the area of job security, can compete and can be effective in the new environment. Certainly, the work of the last ten years in J & J and at Ethicon and with Local 630 has paid off. In the last two years, because of the workoff in inventories in our industry, there has been no growth in Ethicon's business. We have managed to adjust to this and maintain our profit margin without layoffs and give-back bargaining because of the kind of cooperation that has been developed here in Somerville.

Looking to the future, I believe it becomes evident that the need is to continue the cooperation; continue the efforts for flexibility, productivity, and quality; continue to maintain job security; and continue to provide greater job satisfaction. I believe we have at Ethicon, and in Local 630, every reason to feel confident about the future because of the work that we have had underway now for 10 years.

Chapter 4

THE AMALGAMATED CLOTHING & TEXTILE WORKERS UNION ACHIEVEMENT

Mike Shay

The Central and South Jersey Joint Board of the Textile Division of the Amalgamated Clothing & Textile Workers Union (ACTWU) is comprised of 16 different local unions, representing approximately 4,000 members. These members manufacture pillows, curtains, knitted goods, tapes, and health care products. A significant portion of our membership is employed at various facilities of different companies of the Johnson & Johnson Corporation. Local 630 ACTWU is our largest local within the Joint Board and presently has approximately 1,500 members employed at the Johnson & Johnson Products, Johnson & Johnson Products Research, Johnson & Johnson Corporate Headquarters, and at Ethicon, Inc. in Somerville, New Jersey. Ethicon employs approximately 750 of Local 630's membership. The membership has an average age of 42 and an average seniority of between 18 and 20 years. Local 630 has three full-time officers, other part-time officers, and department stewards who have dual responsibilities in the plant as workers and union representatives.

Local 630 has a 40-year bargaining relationship with Johnson & Johnson and has been recognized at Ethicon, Somerville since the plant was built in 1955–1956. It has some of the finest, hard-working, and forward-looking leadership of any union that I have come into contact with during my 18 years of union experience as well as my 11 years with ACTWU.

My experience with the management of Johnson & Johnson has been somewhat schizophrenic. Some of the most heated battles, major disappointments, vehement arguments, legal entanglements, and sheer frustrations of my career have been the result of dealing with Johnson & Johnson, generally and Ethicon, specifically. But I can also state without equivocation that some of the people I respect most in the field of labor relations are employed by Johnson & Johnson and Ethicon. They are talented, honest and, very important, open-minded and flexible. They also have that quality prized above all others in this field: one can accept their word with confidence.

Furthermore, there has been a long history of stable relationships between labor and management, a mature union membership, a progressive union leadership, and an open-minded management operating a profitable company with a stable market.

With these as "givens" one might assume that the idea of instituting a joint labor-management consultative planning and problem-solving process would be relatively easy. After all, it was an essentially simple idea: the most valuable resource a company has is the tremendous reservoir of knowledge possessed by the workers—knowledge of how to solve current productivity and quality related problems, and even more important, how to avoid them in the future. Finally, it might be assumed that management and labor might reach some understanding around the basic issue of guaranteed job security.

How wrong such assumptions could be!

Now, let us start at the beginning. In summer 1980, the management at Ethicon informed the union that they would like to have a work involvement program similar to the one at Johnson & Johnson Products. In exchange for the union's cooperation in such a program, the company was prepared to agree to the same kind of joint policy statement that had been agreed to at Johnson & Johnson Products. This policy statement was finalized and in September 1980, the first policy meeting was held.

In October 1980, training of union and management trainees began. March 1981 saw the beginning of team training. In June 1981, the company agreed to provide a measure of job security so that any job that was rendered unnecessary as a result of productivity improvements through the work involvement program would be protected for up to two years.

It was unfortunate, however, that the union forgot every lesson we had learned through our experience at Johnson & Johnson Products—the need to go slow, to allow people to come to their own conclusions, to consult and attempt to develop consensus.

During this same period, Ethicon also had contracted for a program to evaluate how their managers were spending their time. The conflict between the consultative process of work involvement and the other unilateral program became apparent as the company started requiring workers to keep records on exactly how they spent their time. Stress built up on both supervisors and workers. Workers blamed the Work Involvement process for this stress and the tightening of break, lunch, and other out-of-work area policies.

Shortly after this tightening of policies, discipline was imposed. These issues spilled over into the 1981 negotiations. Despite lengthy discussions, the matters were unresolved, resulting in the union issuing an ultimatum: either the company withdraw the other program or the union would exercise its right to withdraw from the work involvement process. The company refused and on June 29, 1981 the union sent a letter to its membership stating that it was no longer a participant in the Work Involvement process at Ethicon. Understandably, considerable confusion and hard feelings remained after such a confrontation, and the program was dropped during the fall of 1981.

During the summer of 1981, I became manager of the Central and South Jersey Joint Board and Ethicon appointed a new plant manager. After months of discussion among the union leadership, Ethicon plant management, and Participative Systems, Inc. (PSI), we decided to explore the possibility one more time. A total of 17 months after the union withdrew its participation, an off-site meeting took place among plant management, officers and stewards of the local union, and participants from

PSI. This body, after several intense days of discussion, drafted its own charter. For all intent and purposes, we were back in business as of November 1982. By the following January, we saw the next first policy meeting, and we proceeded very cautiously. So cautiously, in fact, that team training did not resume until January 1984, with the first teams graduating in March, 1984. We had the first policy meeting in September 1980 and graduated our first team four years later.

This second start-up was not without its major crisis as well. During the summer of 1983 Ethicon opened a new facility in another part of the country, and ACTWU initiated an organizing campaign shortly thereafter.

It is sufficient to state that it was the union's perception that the company's behavior and attitude were in complete contradiction to what the philosophy of Work Involvement was all about. Several allegations of National Labor Relations Act (NLRA) violations were made by the union, and a number of complaints were issued by the National Labor Relations Board (NLRB). The officers and stewards of Local 630 were very involved in the organizing attempt and, after the loss of the representation election in May 1983, much in-depth soul searching took place. If considered in conjunction with some extremely difficult negotiations for a new contract during May through June 1983, one can readily imagine how close to pulling out once again the union came. In fact, there were several days during this period when I absolutely favored such a decision. Several factors mitigated against that option. They were:

1. The firm belief that the president of the local and I shared, that a better way of doing business with management had to be found. The old way of doing business simply was not working. We had lost more than 200 members in the previous four years.

2. The feeling that this belief was also shared by some members of Ethicon management, such as Clark Leslie and Bob Bury. Clark and Bob were willing to demonstrate their conviction by making an informal commitment that expanded job security principles beyond the point contained in the formal written agreement. Spe-

cifically, they agreed that any future reduction required would be done through attrition, not by layoffs.

3. Some wise counseling by Participative Systems during that crisis. Sid Rubinstein made the point that something was going on with management generally in the country and within Ethicon, specifically. Two different management attitudes toward unions were developing:

    a. Unions have no legitimate role in our society and are to be avoided at all costs. Since this philosophy is purely emotional, it cannot be dealt with logically;

    b. Unions are to be avoided, and organizing campaigns fought, in order to maintain cost effectiveness. This philosophy is based on the concept that non-union facilities simply are more cost-effective to operate than unionized facilities. This attitude, as Sid pointed out, could be changed through evidence and persuasion. We had the opportunity at Ethicon to create an experience and generate a body of data to demonstrate conclusively that unionized facilities are as cost-effective, or even more so, than non-union facilities. In fact, if the work involvement process is to achieve maximum effect, that process must take place between equals. The creative dynamics of conflict and resolution can only take place among equals and, in the workplace, this can only take place where the workers are represented by a union.

This made a great deal of sense. There are many reasons why workers need unions, not simply to be cost-effective, but cost-effective is one argument, I believe, management understands.

Obstacles still remain that not only threaten the success of the program but its survival. These obstacles are voiced as sincere objections to the work involvement process; indeed, objections to the very principles on which the process is based.

It should be noted at this point that our international union does not object to this type of program. In fact, ACTWU has had a fair amount of experience in this type of endeavor with

Xerox. But it is a different experience because of all the different manufacturing facilities of Xerox, in the United States, are organized by ACTWU. That is not the same experience as at Ethicon and Johnson & Johnson. As a result, I believe our top leadership tolerates the program. During our organizing attempt at the new Ethicon facility, a kind of "I told you so" aura was emitted out of union headquarters. But I can tell you also that whenever we've needed help fron the international in terms of getting our own industrial engineer to check figures or take part in cooperative incentive design programs, we had the needed cooperation and support. Within Local 630 there are members whose judgment and opinions over the years I have come to value highly; yet, these very same members warn me that Work Involvement will not—cannot possibly—succeed because of various objections. This is literally how they were stated:

1. The company's attitude toward the union has changed. The company never really fought attempts at organizing in the past. Now they do.
2. The company has opened two non-union plants: one in the South and one in the Southwest. The company will simply transfer all the knowledge that we have provided to the two nonunion operations. We are simply teaching the company how better to eliminate our jobs.
3. The principles of avoiding layoffs are wrong. If we are forced to carry excess people, it affects the right of the senior employees. Seniority is what unions are all about. It affects the rights of the senior employees by:
   a. Impacting on overtime; the excess people fill in for absenteeism which used to be filled by overtime.
   b. The avoidance of layoff limits the number of jobs open for bids. There are senior people waiting to bid into other areas which are not opened up and bid for because they are filled with the excess people.
   c. More temporary transfers are required, resulting in a loss of incentive opportunities for senior people.
   d. The company will be forced to layoff people eventually. When it happens, they will be forced to lay-

off three times as many because of all the excess production. Don't avoid layoffs—lay them off now. "If it was good enough for me 30 years ago, it's good enough for the younger ones today."

4. This company's not ready for cooperation or Work Involvement. Look what is happening to the crafts. The company took away their annual inequity increases, cut back on the number of machinists in the central shop, cut down on their overtime, won't compromise on subcontracting issues; yet they want cooperation. Cooperation is supposed to be a two-way street.

5. We know what the company really wants and that is to put as many people on the street as possible. They want to replace us with robots, automatic winders, automatic packaging machines, automated warehouses. This is not Work Involvement—it is war.

6. Unions are not supposed to be concerned with productivity, quality, or the competitive posture of the company. This work involvement process is an attempt to destroy the union. The company tries to make people feel guilty about seniority, overtime, and other fringe benefits—about earning higher wages. They're trying to prepare people for no wage increase at all or concession bargaining; in fact, to destroy the loyalty our people feel to the union by making the union take the blame for what is going wrong.

There were a host of other objections as well. But these were the most serious and the most frequently mentioned. They were serious for two very important reasons: they were expressed by people who had spent the better part of their working lives building the union; and, because each one of the aforementioned objections contains some element of truth.

The company's attitude toward the union organizing presently non-union operations has certainly changed. Ethicon, Somerville, has experienced a decline of almost 200 jobs in the past four years. The company, because of competitive pressures, is much less flexible on workload, workrule, overtime, and other similar grievances than I have been led to believe they were in the past. Automation is a threat, and cooperative programs have been used by some companies as a union-busting device.

I do not know how to explain away these strongly held, strongly voiced objections. But I do know this—that we are proud of the program; we believe in it. We share the belief that a better alternative to the old pattern of labor-management relations must be found because the old methods alone no longer work. If any management person doubts this premise, he should ponder the fate of our stereo, television, home video, small appliance, sewing machine, steel, and auto industries. If any union person doubts that premise, he should ponder declining membership roles, declining percentages of union workers as a percentage of the total labor force, increased demands for union-sponsored social services and the present crisis in collective bargaining. It results largely, I believe, from the collapse or near collapse, or certainly dire straits, of the previously mentioned industries.

I have no doubt that the better way of doing business is by developing a joint consultative process of labor-management planning and problem-solving.

Part III

PERSPECTIVE

Chapter 5

GREATER INDUSTRIAL DEMOCRACY

Sam Camens

I believe most of us agree with Sid Rubinstein: what a great democratic society, industrial complex, and union movement we would have in America *if* we could actually organize and put into effect the kind of relationship that would guarantee American products would be of the highest quality in the world and that American workers would have a feeling of employment security. I should even go further and say, "There's more to it." There are greater reasons why the union movement is supporting labor-management participation teams, as we view them within the Steelworker's Union. I believe they've got to be coupled with a general approach toward quality and employment security. I agree with all of that. That is how we look at this from a union point of view and from a social point of view.

American industry must understand that it has to democratize the industrial complexes if we are going to remain a democratic society. I don't say that lightly. I say that with great concern because I believe that one of the great problems we have in America is that the trade union movement must be considered an integral part of our democratic society, as there can be no democratic society without a free trade union movement. Everybody has to understand that. In reality, unions are not accepted totally; we are tolerated and that is one of the great problems we have in moving forward with labor-management participation teams. We must always question—"Is this a ploy of management to somehow weaken the labor movement?" In the Steelworkers' Union we fret about that. If we believe we have a decent relationship with the company, we believe that through the process, we can develop an even better relationship.

One of the basic problems is that, even if we accept the fact that we are a democratic society, by-and-large, we only practice it about half the time each day—maybe not even that much. Everybody works the major part of their lives. I know what has taken up most of my life—it has been work.

You find, as you enter an industrial complex, that there is the equivalent of a big sign that is not written, but is understood and everybody knows it when they walk through the plant gates. It says, "democracy stops here." There is no question about it. Workers do not have any rights to solve their problems. They do not have any rights to say anything beyond what has been written into a contract, and the basic running of the plant is totally autocratic from top management on down. That's how it has been in American industry, and in many ways, it has served us well.

We have built a great industrial complex, but times are changing, and the American work force better begin to understand what is happening in America. There is going to be great conflict between what has happened in the past and the attitude of workers in America today. As my kids always say to me, no matter how much I argue with them because I do not always understand the problem—they said, "Dad, I want to enjoy work." Work must have some kind of social fulfillment. In order to have that, you must have some kind of feeling that you are involved and can create and give something to the job, not just continue to take orders. In the past, American industrial organizations have been built around so-called "scientific management." That is to say, you took orders—you were told when, how, and what to do. Every job was broken down to its smallest integral part. That is the way steel plants were managed.

What is important to understand is that what developed from that cultural relationship was the general perception that you have to watch a worker; that he cannot be trusted, that you must have a foreman on his back because he is irresponsible. Also, if you have to tell him how to do everything, he is dumb. He cannot learn. I am not exaggerating. That is the perception of what an American worker is, and that is how he is treated in a plant, and that is our problem. It is our problem in industrial relations and is our problem in quality and production. That is the basic problem with everything that is happening in the American industrial complex.

From that attitude flowed a whole relationship—a relationship of distrust, of alienation; a relationship of building layer-upon-layer of management; a relationship where everybody of importance required a specialist and anything that required ability required specialized training. Somehow, there had to be a specialist, a department, and a standard procedure. From all of that, there developed an inability to actually resolve problems—not only from the point of view of refusing to give the workers the right to use their experience, knowledge, and intuition to resolve problems, but also an overexpanded management with bureaucratic control. If you had to have layer-upon-layer of people to watch workers, you had to have layer-upon-layer of management to watch management. It all flows from the same perceptions.

Instead of actually reaching the point where we could work and resolve problems in the most efficient way, we found that every time we had a problem in the plant it was lost in communications. Why is it that most quality problems were never solved in the steel industry? Simply because it was impossible to talk to the so-called specialists, and they never understood the problems. Workers were told to "ship it." That was the standard answer: "ship it." Because of America's position in the steel market at that given moment, you could sell anything in the world, and the main concern was to get it out and not be concerned with the quality of the steel.

I suppose you'd be surprised and amazed if I were to tell you that, since we initiated the LMPT program in some plants, we are correcting things that had existed for 40, 50, even 75, years during which nobody did a damn thing about it. I'm not exaggerating.

For example, at one plant, can you believe that after 40 years of running a strip mill, coils had soft centers; when you stacked them up three or four high, they caved in? Loose bands on the end of the coil had to be burned off because the banders could not band them physically. Oil spots on the cold roll product had existed since the plant was opened, and nobody did anything about it. And yet, when the LMPT teams were formed, one of the first things they wanted to do—which was an amazing thing in that plant—was to get rid of the soft centers, the loose bands and the oil spots on the coils. It meant a savings of $2 million a year between prime product and secondary product for which they had been sold because of the great amount of scrap that was generated. You can go through plant after plant on that theme.

You may think that I am rawing it; maybe putting on a good bush act. The truth of it is that in this same plant there is no longer an LMPT process today. That is the reality of the times; reality because the relationship between the company and the union has deteriorated to such an extent. This same plant, however, had put into place a cost-effective plan which would have allowed up to 10 percent extra people at that mill during production downturns. This 10 percent of the otherwise laid off work force would work on problem-solving and training rather than be laid off. This provision was part of the LMPT process at this plant. This approach helped stabilize employment and use downturns to develop a more effective production process.

After four or five years of LMPT, I have great concern whether we are going to make it. Are we going to make the changes that we discuss here? When I went out in the hall and talked with a few of our union people, I asked, "What was your perception of what Sid said; what do you think?" They answered, "Great! Boy, if we could only do it;" "I have doubts. I don't think my membership would accept it." "What do you mean, your membership wouldn't accept it?" I believe the membership would *NOT* accept it because you know as well as I do what Sid is talking about. I have had long discussions with Sid.

He is talking about doing away with layoffs. Our people *want* lay-offs; our people want a vacation; they want unemployment insurance; they want SUB. The thing that concerns me is that nobody should misunderstand the gravity and importance of this issue. What we are talking about is a basic cultural change.

Unemployment Insurance and SUB are a part of our cultural life. It is an accepted approach to unemployment in America, but does nothing about solving it or coming to grips with it from the point of view of the great destruction it creates. In the end, in spite of what workers think of it, SUB and unemployment are the things that bother them all their lives. They cannot move on from a job like basic management. Their legs are tied to a job once they earn tenured service. They don't plan to leave because their pension and benefit rights are tied to that plant and their unemployment rights as well.

The greatest tragedy is what happens to an American worker when his plant shuts down, and this is reality in the steel industry today. That is the reality in all the industrial plants of America today. And what are the basic reasons? Sid has pointed out one reason, because we're not competing from a quality point of view on the international market. A related problem tied to competing on the quality front is how to enhance employment security as a goal of LMPT. It is a long-range problem. I don't think we can build LMPT teams to last unless every worker who wants to participate gets a chance to and, at the same time, feels his employment security is being enhanced, not diminished. That is the important part of LMPT and why we support it.

But if we are making the plant more efficient and his long-time security is not tied to that efficiency in the end, he is going to become distrustful of the process because his job is at stake again. As union leaders and business leaders, we must understand that. As leaders, we have the responsibility, from a long-term point of view, to re-evaluate our position on layoffs. We must evaluate it in terms of how do we keep people working and not in terms of how do we pay them to take time off. If it is time off, you cut the work week, or you find other means of doing that, but not layoff to the point where his job is at stake.

The Japanese have resolved this problem, and it is not as

simple as basing it on the terms of an LMPT relationship. I believe that this is our problem. It also translates itself into the union-company negotiating relationship. They are both tied together. From that point of view, we must understand that we must tie in the whole training and problem-solving processes and keep these people at work through LMPT by planning for it. I have no problem with that. We have done it. We must rethink our whole negotiating posture and figure out how to deal with the problem. The problem is that it is tied up in governmental and social decisions and it cannot be separated. So we are dealing with a problem of great magnitude which encompasses the total thinking in this country. This is very noticeable in Japan. I have made three trips to Japan and have seen evidence of this fact.

Once we met with a Japanese Productivity Committee and I had a little argument with them. They asked, "What do you think the number one responsibility of management is?" Well, I know what the answer is in this country. It is management of money. It is not management of the steel plants anymore. Management's primary responsibility is money. That is the American outlook.

In Japan, we were told, the number one responsibility of management is to continue to expand the company and find jobs for their workers. I kept asking, "You mean it isn't the profits you make? It isn't the handling of capital?" And they said, "No, that is secondary." And that is a difference in cultural attitude. And you see it there. They talk about how they expand and how they can get into new industry. I haven't talked to a steel company representative in the last 15 years that said they were expanding into new industry and creating new jobs. When we sit down with our steel people they talk about how they are losing money, not how they are expanding into new fields. It is how do you contract out work and shut down what plant. That's the way we do it. Why do you shut down one plant? You know the answer: to take the capital losses in any one year and write them off against the last seven years. We are learning all about this now because of all the plant shutdowns we have been involved in and the tragedies that result.

When we talk about quality, let me say that management has

never let us be part of quality. Now they are beginning to understand that you can't legislate quality; you can't order quality; and you can't hide it in the specialists' rooms. You can go through a plant and there are banners all over: "Quality is First"—all kinds of slogans. They hire consultants who give them another slogan, and somehow that is going to do it. Every time there is a new manager, he comes in with another slogan that promises to attack quality from another angle. How you attack quality is very simple. Make it a part of every worker's responsibility.

I said very simple, but it isn't that simple because of our cultural past. We have never let workers handle quality. Their jobs were broken down into individual functions and responsibilities. And now, when you give them new responsibilities, they rebel and say, "It was never part of my job, and I don't want it. It's not my job class." This is what the union did when we organized. We took the plants as we found them and organized them, and we institutionalized the process on a fair and equitable basis. That was our job. And that is part of our problem. Don't minimize it.

The union must now realize that if we are going to compete on an international basis, there have to be great changes in our plants. We must make quality part of our job. We must be a part of the process of change; that is our new responsibility.

Now we take on this new responsibility with the understanding that if we are going to function as a good union we have some responsibility for the viability of the company. Management has to realize that if we are to assume responsibility, management prerogatives that were never clearly defined anyway, are not so precious. And they are not! We have a joint responsibility to keep a company viable. All of these things that we were never allowed to talk about and workers did not have anything to say about are things that must now be shared to make the proper decisions.

We have piles of reports in my office of what workers have done because they were given the responsibility to do it. You can't believe what they have transformed, what changes they have made to equipment and quality and how eager they are to do so. Management must understand that once they make a decision to develop Labor-Management Participation Teams, what these teams propose are not just suggestions to management.

Management must understand that if they do not implement them and implement them immediately, those teams will fall apart. There must be a sharing of the power of decision-making that used to be the foreman's job. The teams will want to do things that in the past were completely controlled by the old bureaucrats. As an example, I recently attended a meeting where one of the companies is putting in LMPTs in a very different way. They are not dealing with quality. The LMPT teams say, "We have to begin to look at quality." And they ask, "How are we going to do it?" Management has not given them any ideas on what to do.

The LMPT team said, "Why don't we call in the buyer and the salesman from a company that buys most of our products and sit down and have a discussion with them and ask them what they think of the product they are buying from us?"

That is what they did. They brought in their customer who gave his criticism and their comment was, "Well, nobody ever told us that. We didn't know it." You hide it from the very guy who produces it. Some buyers and salesmen do this. The team decided to do it again with another customer, and they went systematically through this procedure for a rolling mill. They did it on their own initiative, not on management's suggestion, and now it is expanding. Now they are saying, "What about statistical control. Can we be taught that?"

The great surprise about statistical control is that you don't have to be a college graduate to learn it. Now that there are computers, you don't have to give all the charts fancy names. Program the computer, put in the material and it will give you the end points and the chart with one flick of a button. That is how simplified it has become. Workers want to use it but with one understanding—that it is not used to measure the performance of workers. They want computers to point out what the defects are in quality. Give them that kind of understanding and see how they gobble up statistical control and make corrections to what goes on in the plant and what they can do about it. That is important. It is a basic change of attitude. It is a scientific approach to the control of quality on the floor with the people who are in control of quality.

I want to mention that we have a problem with our mid-management and our mid-union people. We have to find ways to involve them. Where this hasn't been done, we are in trouble. Mid-management people resist it. They see their power sapped. They do not understand their new role. Management people should plan for the future of new products and work out problems that exist in the plant instead of the redundant roles they now play in the plant performing functions that can be done in half the time by subordinates. Some of our stewards and mid-management people started talking with each other and one of the management people said, "It's about time you talked to me. I've been waiting for this. I know this is going on in the plant. Nobody's bothered to inform me of what's going on below me." I believe this is what people must understand. If you believe you can build a process of developing teams on the floor in problem-solving, and do nothing else within the organization and still reap the benefits, you are in a dream world. You will receive three or four years out of it and some real value, I'll agree. But at the end of three or four years, it will break up because the organization has not changed in total. If you're talking about building a participative system among foremen, understand that you must change the total management system to a participative one. If you believe a general foreman will sit down and develop a participative system with the people he works with and still receive the autocratic rule from above, he will rebel at this non-participation in decision-making above him, and he should. You will have the same bureaucratic stumbling you had before because you are talking about total participation and total group dynamics, if you wish to develop an efficient system of operation. I suppose this is difficult to take from a union representative—a kind of management lecture. But, it happens to be how we see the process, and it happens to be true. We have much to learn. I do not want to be critical of management. We have to learn as a union. We have to develop participative management. We are thinking about it and trying to do it, but it hasn't been totally successful because it isn't easy to change cultural relationships that have gone on for years. Some of us are insisting on it and we will do something about that because it is part of the changing world in which we live.

The whole future is ahead of us. Everything is changing before us and I believe the key to it all is that we must be able to understand the need for change. I don't think anybody changes unless they consciously understand the need, and plan for it. If we plan, and if we do it on a joint basis because it cannot be done alone, we have a chance of success—a far better chance than any other country in the world. I have never seen a group of workers who are more intelligent, more knowledgeable, or with greater eagerness and initiative, and who want to get involved, than the American worker. There is nothing passive about them, believe me. When they don't agree, they are a tough bunch to handle; but convince them that there is an effort of real joint participation and there can be a basic change in American industry that will be the salvation of our competitive position in the world today.

Chapter 6

THE DECLINE OF THE AUTHORITARIAN TRADITION

Lynn Williams

The talents of workers are America's single greatest unused resource. In the work force, we have people of intelligence and creativity who have a great desire to do things. In large measure, they have been shut out of the system, unable to use their talents or work to their full potential. The workers are the greatest unused resource in our society.

The authoritarian structure we have built in the industrial, enterprising part of our society, and also throughout our society, is in contradiction. Although we preach democratic values and educate our children to be critical in their judgments, to be well-informed, and to exercise their initiative; we then usher them into a society which traditionally, in almost all of its institutions, is authoritarian. It is a "top down" society—a fundamental contradiction of the philosophy we espouse about our government and society in general.

This has led to some very difficult situations including the rejection of workers and their ideas. It has also led to the rejection of trade unionism. Authoritarianism has attacked the trade union and views it as the most significant and effective challenge launched against it in an institutional and traditional sense. The basic contradiction between the authoritarian ideas, which run much of our society, and the democracy we preach, is in many ways exemplified in the traditional struggle between corporations and business which seek to prevent the labor movement from pursuing its goals of greater worker involvement, that is, the opportunity to express their concerns and needs.

The entire authoritarian aspect and where it originated, like everything else in life, has its pluses and minuses. Authoritarianism is positive in the sense that it has produced our dynamic society: the whole principle of entrepreneurship—the American idea that we can all do anything; potentially, we can all own our own businesses. We can all use as much energy, dynamism, and creativity as we can muster. This leads to the concept that I can do exactly as I see fit. This is one of the elements that has led to extreme authoritarianism. This philosophy might be appropriate at a mom and pop store but not in enormous corporate structures. But authoritative rule in modern corporations is a myth for no one in the corporation is an owner. Everybody involved in running General Motors or U.S. Steel is an employee of the company. Yet, these myths persist.

The positive aspect of that entrepreneurial, dynamic ideal has contributed enormously to the material success of our society. What makes Americans so sensitive about too much government intervention is the fear that, somehow, it will interfere with that dynamic.

The challenge is how we can unleash that entrepreneurial energy and tradition from the authoritarian mold. How we can weld it to the democratic principles of our society and, thereby, find a new dynamism that is relevant to the real world in which we live, a world of large corporations and large structures? Very few are mom and pop shops; very few are examples of that traditional entrepreneurial ideal. In our society that ideal has a lot of strength and character; it carries a lot of emotional weight, touching almost all classes of people.

It appears there is a way to consolidate this and appeal to the entrepreneurial urge in all of us. We all want to be creative, forceful, and influential. We all want to accomplish something. One of the most exciting avenues is available to us, allowing us to weld these traditional values into organizational and institutional approaches in terms of the objectives of both corporations and unions, and the objectives of government institutions. These ideas have a very broad application. There is a way to mold these things together and inject a new dynamism and creativity into our whole society.

In past years, none of this mattered very much because the American economy was so successful. It was the biggest and most powerful country in the world without any significant challenge. In a sense, America carried the rest of the world. We could afford the luxury of fighting with each other, challenging each other and shutting down our industries for months. None of it had much impact. We do not live in that kind of a world anymore. It has changed dramatically. There are many things that many of us believe ought to be done about that change, both in terms of inhibiting some of its excesses and finding new ways to roll with the change. But I believe only the blind among us would suggest that the change is not occurring. The change requires new concern and new concepts. The old ways are not adequate. The old luxury of challenging each other on any subject and accepting whatever social discord and disruption resulted does not make any sense in the world in which we find ourselves today. We cannot afford it.

I am not pessimistic about the future of this country and its economy—far from it. I believe that we are on the brink of a whole new growth in the level of wealth, production, and development of a society that will achieve accomplishments, as we did in the 1930s. People who had talked about futurists in the 1930s might well have concluded that the world was about to come to an end in the 1940s, and, in a sense, it nearly did. But, in another sense, we were on the edge of the greatest spurt of economic and industrial development and production of wealth the world has ever seen. There is no reason to believe this isn't the case today. The question, of course, is how do we get there; that is, within the framework of traditional authoritarianism and the impact it has had in terms of the rejection of workers, and trade unionism specifically? I'd like to confess that I have a dream. To be realistic, it is a dream I do not believe I am going to see realized. But it would be very constructive if we could stop fighting about the union's right to exist. If only it could simply be understood that unions are acceptable and are a reasonable way for us to do our business. It is only reasonable that as larger aggregations of employees are working for corporations or government that they should have some process of collective representation. Trade unions provide this, by and large, in a responsible way.

The dream could begin to be realized the minute trade unionism is accepted, the minute we stop expending the enormous energy we waste on both sides in conducting this continuing warfare: whether unions will exist, will expand, and if they will be in the south or the southwest. These questions will be moot. If we were to use that energy to make our system work and stop fighting each other about a fundamental institution like trade unionism, a whole world of opportunities would open up. It would be a world in which I should like to live. I don't expect that I will. I don't have illusions about that because the reality is that some of the attitudes are too deeply ingrained. What some people perceive to be the economic imperatives to fight unions are so established that I am afraid I don't see us overcoming that.

As a union leader, how does one deal with that? On the one hand, we would like to see union acceptance, involvement, the unleashing of all of this energy; we would like to move into a more participatory mode. But on the other hand, economic warfare exists whenever we try to organize a new plant, even with people with whom we have fine collective bargaining relations, often one of long standing. How do we deal with this in terms of leadership? I have agonized over this. I have been interested in the Quality of Work Life process for ten years, and have tried in quiet ways to see what I could do to encourage it in one place or another. Preaching labor-management cooperation is not a great political platform for election in the labor movement. Our union elections are more vigorous and noisy than any other major union. And, so, if you are in the process of seeking to win an election, as I have been, you have to decide on your program. Labor-management cooperation is not the greatest program. On the other hand, if that is what you really believe in and that is where you believe the future rests, you must try to be honest with yourself and the people with whom you are dealing.

I have grappled with this, and I have come to the conclusion that what we are really doing is espousing two conflicting ideas. We are letting corporate America know that if they want a row with us, they are in for the damndest fight they have ever seen. We will go out after their unorganized members and will take them on in collective bargaining struggles. We will be just as adversarial as we know how to be—if that is the way they want to play the game. We will use all the considerable resources and talents that we've developed in our institution over many years of adversarial conduct. We will use all of these just as effectively as we can manage.

But, we also want to send another message to corporate America: we do not necessarily believe this is the best way. We believe there are more creative and constructive ways to deal with this problem. We want to work with those who are interested and willing; because we, the United Steelworkers, are willing and I hope we can say the same for the labor movement. We are willing whenever a corporation wants to try something more rational, more creative, more constructive. We are willing whenever a corporation wants to invite our members to use their ideas and initiative to move beyond traditional adversarial conflicts.

I tried out this pitch for the first time with most of the members of our international executive board. I was astounded at how positively it was received and what clear note of agreement it seemed to strike. Everbody said, "Okay, if we've got to fight we'll fight, but if we want to do it in a better way or a more constructive way, then we should be willing and prepared to do that." We had not been pursuing this particular pitch. We made it union policy at our recent convention, and it was well received there. We have not had enough experience with it to make any judgments. But it appears there is an application here in the local union arena. I believe we are moving into new modes of dealing with companies. We have to make sure our members understand we are not giving up any of our contractual responsibilities as their advocates and representatives.

Looking back at the history of labor-management relations, the idea of a friendly, non-adversarial, cooperative relationship with "The Boss" is what concerns and frightens some of our members. They are afraid they may lose the rights, protection, and security they spent so many years in establishing. It is this kind of security the members expect the union to provide. If we can assure them that we will continue to provide it, and continue to be their staunch advocates; vigorously pursuing their interests while at the same time working cooperatively with management, then I believe we can move forward.

We are very tough-minded about this in the Steelworkers. We are interested in trying to proceed with these kinds of projects without the commitment of management to accept their implications. We are prepared to let it be a developing commitment. But I do not believe this movement will succeed in America, except where there is trade union representation. That is why I am not afraid of it. Many trade unionists are afraid it will be used as an anti-union tool, a way of subverting the labor movements. I am more inclined to see it as a way of building the labor movement. I believe any company that starts on a participative process, honestly and conscientiously, with a non-union group will inevitably move in the direction of organization and some kind of collective effort. I also believe that a company that tries to do it honestly will be faced with some very tough situations in which they will either have to reassert the old authoritarian values which will destroy the system, or they will need some other mechanism to solve those problems. There are still some problems, however, which I believe can be solved best only by the collective bargaining process.

To put it very simply, what we are trying to do here is increase the economic pie. This process does not resolve the questions about how you divide the economic pie. I am a great believer in collective bargaining as the only process, consistent with democratic values of our society in which that economic pie can be divided. I will make this prediction: that this cooperative movement will not exist 15 to 20 years from now unless it is a joint management-trade union kind of exercise. It will not exist in 15 to 20 years unless there is a commitment from the top leadership of both institutions.

I see this process as fundamental. The same principles of participation, the same principles of consensus, the same principles of providing security to both sides of the table—all these principles have national application. If these mechanisms could operate on a national basis solving some of our national problems, they could make a great contribution. But I do not believe this process can ultimately survive unless there is commitment to work in support of this kind of approach by the top leadership of both the operations and the trade union movement.

Prior to our international convention, we had a meeting of all our local unions involved in Labor-Management Participation Teams, as we call them in the Steelworkers. For the first time, we gathered all our people from various companies. I said that the future we believed in was in that room; that if we were going to grapple effectively with the challenges America faces, which our whole industrial relations systems faces, the future depends on whether this cooperative approach can be developed, expanded, and institutionalized—whether it can become the way in which we do our work together.

Chapter 7

WORKER PARTICIPATION THEN AND NOW

John Hoerr

It has become common in recent years for detractors of the work process called "participation" to criticize it from Olympian points of view. As seen from one high bluff, participation is no more than an embroidery of pop sociological concepts surrounding the *old* labor-management cooperation approach. The expounders of this view invariably cite the cooperative efforts of World Wars I and II and scattered projects in the 1920s as examples of the *old* that should give pause to anyone who would be so foolish as to cooperate today. "Old," in this context, also means "tired," as if ideas—like humans—wear out with age and, after a short life, should be put out of their misery. Another view from the precipice sets forth what might be called the "merely" argument. Worker participation in the United States is *merely* an imitation of Japanese forms of labor-management cooperation—although (here is the amusing irony of it) the United States has already lost the competitive race with Japan. Alternatively, hold the merelies, all joint efforts are *merely* fear-driven reactions to various adversities, such as recessions, deregulation, and rising imports, and will fade away at the first sign of returning prosperity.

There is something to be said for each of these views. All of the major elements of current worker participation efforts (problem-solving by teams of workers, for example, or autonomous work groups) have been tried in the past, sometime, somewhere. Many American companies have copied Japanese techniques, some experiencing good results and some—those who thought of it as injecting Japanese blood into an American arm —discovering that cloning has succeeded only in science fiction. It may turn out to be the case that many of the work reforms of recent years, undertaken during hard times, will disappear in good times. On the other hand, Christianity, American-style democracy, and the substitution of long pants for knee-length breeches and silk stockings, managed to survive the relatively better times that succeeded their formative years.

Later in this chapter, I shall briefly trace the history of labor-management cooperation in the United States to support my contention that the above truisms do not arise out of an objective examination of practices. Rather, they exist as states of mind trapped in ideological cul-de-sacs. They reflect rigid beliefs about the behavior of economic man but tell us nothing about the present situation of worker participation. That is what this book does.

The Leadership Conference of 1984 demonstrated to me, as an observer, that worker participation no longer consists primarily of theories spun by intellectuals. It exists as real, down-to-earth processes in many hundreds of factories, mines and offices. The Olympian mindsets that feed on the false beliefs of worker participation wither in the face of actual descriptions of the process by workers and managers. One could see, in microcosm, the evolutionary process by which change has occurred in the concepts and practices that have constituted state-of-the-art over the last 75 years in the general area of labor-management cooperation and specifically, worker participation. I was impressed by the honesty and open-mindedness of the workers, managers, and union officials who attended the conference. It is always exciting to see people literally learning as they talk to one another—and this often happens when actual workers and supervisors tell of their experiences in a participative process. This conference had an additional dimension: union officials and managers on both sides of the labor-management table gave bold insights into their fears, doubts, and hopes for worker participation.

A few examples will suffice. On the second day of the conference, Lynn Williams, president of the United Steelworkers, sat in front of the group in his shirt sleeves and spoke extemporaneously, aided by a few notes, on a sensitive issue. Many union leaders, if they must declare their position on worker participation, either condemn it as a scheme used by management to exploit workers or speak tepidly in its favor, with many qualifications and caveats. Williams not only expressed strong support for participation but also proposed a new way of looking at labor-management cooperation.

The American entrepreneurial spirit, Williams said, has done much good for the society. It also has spawned considerable authoritarianism in management. Would it not make sense, he said, to combine that spirit with the creativity of American workers to "find a new dynamism that is appropriate to the real world in which we live?" One senses that Williams was thinking his ideas through as he talked, that he was holding a dialogue with the audience. This is, in its best sense, the participative mode: putting out ideas and hoping to stimulate a dialogue that, in the end, might change long-held attitudes or produce a sudden insight on solving a tough logistical or technical problem.

Another example of the openness of the discussions came during a question and answer period after Clark Leslie, operations vice-president of the Ethicon Division of Johnson & Johnson, had described a participative program at Ethicon's Somerville, New Jersey plant. Leslie was deeply committed to a joint effort with the Amalgamated Clothing & Textile Workers Union, despite the neutral attitude of top corporate people at J & J. One saw the program had succeeded partly because Leslie did not believe that management was the fountain of all industrial wisdom; he was more than willing to listen to the suggestions of rank-and-file workers. This was borne out by his reaction when one of several Ethicon employees in the audience told an embarrassing anecdote about old Ethicon management practices. This woman was a production worker and steward in an operation that turned out suture needles. For years, she said, supervisors had blamed workers for defects in the needles as they came off the production line. Quality control inspectors could easily discover flaws in finished needles by examining them through an "eye loop," a type of magnifying glass that enlarged the needle by a power of 10. But the operators who produced the needles were not supplied with eye loops and, thus, lacked the one piece of equipment that might have helped them turn out flawless needles. "You'd be surprised," the Ethicon worker said, "but for years we asked why didn't the workers have eye loops, and we never got a good answer." They were finally provided only after workers made their case in the work involvement program. Leslie listened to the anecdote, shook his head and said with considerable sarcasm: "Looking through eye loops, you see, has always been a management function."

The examples above illustrate two aspects of the same trend. For the more advanced union and management leaders, worker participation is far more than just another productivity program imposed by the company on the workers and administered by a bureaucracy of clerks. It is a joint process run by the union and the company, with voluntary participants, in a spirit of producing permanent change in the way companies manage people, in the way workers relate to supervisors, and in the way that unions relate to managements. Yet there is great confusion in the field between what is significant change and what is surface change. Sidney Rubinstein, and others like him, have steadily improved their techniques and ideas and moved toward significant, permanent change in the industrial relations system— at least on the shop floor, and in some cases at the corporate level. This cannot be said of many other situations where participation "programs" are installed by rote, without deep roots, without training, and without a commitment by management to allow workers a representative voice in company affairs above the shop-floor level.

Worker participation should not be thought of as a "program" with a finite period of life, but a continuing "processs." The process differs from plant to plant, department to department within a plant, and from team to team within a department because different personalities (with their different mix of talents and ways of thinking) and different problems produce different group dynamics.

For these reasons, participation is not easily definable and certainly defies easy labeling. No one has coined a generic term that is a perfect blend of the general and the concrete, possibly because the concept, unfortunately, is foreign to industrial relations practices in the United States. Into that vacuum have rushed a plethora of not-quite-right terms trailing peculiar acronyms: quality of working life (QWL), quality circle (QC), employee involvement (EI), labor-management participation team (LMPT), employee participation group (EPG), social-technical systems (STS), labor-management committee (LMC).

Some terms, like "autonomous work team," refer to a fairly specific way of organizing work; such a team is a self-directed group of production workers who plan their own activity, assign work internally, and promote group members according to skills learned. Other terms, like "participation," are as broad as life itself (and no one knows how to distinguish "worker participation" from "management participation"). For compulsive classifiers of human behavior under general rubric, there are the familiar "worker democracy," "shop-floor democracy," and the century-old "industrial democracy."

What do these terms mean in any given situation? They mean whatever those who use them want them to mean, and there is no industry standard to which all worker participation efforts must conform. To what degree has the movement infiltrated American industry? The answers are vague, but here are some indications.

A Conference Board survey in 1983 showed that problem-solving committees of workers and supervisors had been set up in 340 (60.7 percent) of 504 selected companies. These companies, however, probably ranked above average in the breadth of their human resource programs. In a 1982 study that was more representative of U.S. experience, the New York Stock Exchange found that about 25 percent of all corporations with 500 or more employees had a human resource "activity" which involved rank-and-file workers in decision-making. The broadest survey to date reporting from the employee point of view was made in 1985 by Sirota and Alper Associated Inc., a New York firm specializing in employee surveys. The firm contacted a representative sample of 2,000 American workers in all industries and all regions. A total of 36 percent of the sample group reported that their companies had formal involvement programs (other than suggestion box plans), and 23 percent said they were personally involved in such a program.[1]

Because of definitional problems, these numbers are far from satisfactory. But they seem to indicate that some form of worker participation is going on at a large number of workplaces. The many concepts have evolved along many lines, throwing up many ways of resolving difficult conceptual and institutional problems inherent in allowing management and labor to work together.

That is why this book is important. The opening chapter by Sidney Rubinstein, one of the pioneers of the modern worker participation movement, is invaluable as a candid history of one consultant's progress in planning and implementing participative programs over a period of 25 years. Rubinstein readily admits that his present concept of worker participation, its theory and structure, did not spring fullgrown from his mind 25 years ago. It evolved over that period out of practical experience. His background as a skilled machinist, tool-and-die maker, trained sociologist and expert on statistical quality control techniques makes him uniquely qualified to approach the technical and social problems of participation. Long before terms like "quality of working life" and "employee involvement" had been invented, Rubinstein was working with unions and management to reform the workplace.

That his efforts sometimes were unsuccessful, or did not have the staying power of a revolution, is all the more reason to listen to what he has to say. Rubinstein, in his own retrospective judgment, made some mistakes. These were sometimes conceptual in nature, sometimes "political" (on occasion he was too bold, on occasion too cautious, in nudging unions and managements to take certain actions). Out of this long experience, however, he and his associates at Participative Systems, Inc. have devised what they believe to be the framework for successful participation. It is not the only possible framework. Other experts in the field stress different elements.

Rubinstein's three-tier structure, however, has the potential of resolving the myriad problems of reforming work in a complex industrial organization. It consists of problem-solving teams on the shop floor, a higher level of committees of middle-management supervisors and union representatives, and steering groups jointly run by company and union officials at the plantwide level. As Rubinstein says, the middle tier involves the crucial general foremen, department superintendents, technical people and union committeemen who most often are left out of participative structures, almost always to the detriment of the process. The three-tier structure is crucial to Rubinstein's insistence that quality assurance must involve all employees at all stages of production. He is right in attacking the traditional quality control system, which is managed exclusively by technical specialists. This is a self-limiting system, which promotes the idea that only professionals have the ability to solve quality problems.

In addition to prescribing this structure, Rubinstein emphasizes employment security and avoiding layoffs as a necessary precondition to obtaining workers' commitment to changes in technology and eliminating onerous work rules. Through this linkage, employment stability benefits both the worker and the employer.

Participative Systems, Inc. is also refreshingly honest about the goals of worker participation. In some of the early QWL efforts of the 1970s, the assumption was that improving the labor-relations climate and providing better washroom and parking facilities would make workers "happy" and eventually lead to increased productivity. Management and labor officials feared that stressing an economic payoff would convince workers that they were being asked to suggest ways off eliminating their own jobs. To no one's surprise, some workers did feel that way. In the steel industry, for example, the acronym LMPT (for Labor-Management Participation Team) was said by critics to really mean Lower Men Per Turn. Rubinstein, however, confronts this problem head on. He believes—and the evidence seems to bear him out—that the large majority of workers want to become more involved in managing the workplace for what might be called economic reasons: to improve product quality and reduce production costs and thus make their company more viable. In his system, the twin goals of making work more productive, as well as more satisfying, are stressed from the outset.

Rubinstein, and others like him, have moved participation onto fairly solid ground by developing practical principles for training people for the process, implementing it and sustaining it. In its most successful forms, participation today is altogether different from the first feeble cooperative efforts of the early twentieth century, and even from the partly naive and idealistic attempts of only a decade ago. To support this thesis, I shall recount briefly some of the major developments in the evolution of worker participation and labor-management cooperation. Although the latter term is more inclusive than participation, the two are often used synonomously.

It should go without saying that some degree of cooperation between workers and managers exists in every workplace. Cooperation among individuals for the common good is the natural state of affairs and has been, if experts on early subhuman and human species are correct, for a few million years. In nineteenth century America, the Industrial Revolution quite suddenly began to convert a largely, rural nation with an ethos of individualism into a largely, urban society of undifferentiated factory workers. The clash of customs and values between the new society of mass production and the old society of farmers, artisans, and small shopkeepers caused immense social, economic, and political problems that, in a sense, are still with us. Long before the Civil War, reformers of all sorts were orating, writing, and wagging their heads about "the labor problem," a term that encompassed characterizations as diverse as man versus machine, labor versus capital, and the proletariat versus the capitalist class. It also referred to the miserable living conditions in industrial slums.

In the workshops, the changing organization of work divided the interests of the owner-manager from those of the artisan-worker. As small, artisan-based firms gradually expanded into giants of mass production, the natural cooperation between owner and one or two skilled, principal employees turned into an authoritarian relationship. As new production technology mushroomed, employers had to find a way to marry machines and manpower so that skilled workers could no longer control the content of jobs and the pace of work.

The answer was provided by Frederick W. Taylor, the engineer who led the "scientific management" movement in the late 1800s and early 1900s. He preached the gospel of fragmentation, dividing production jobs into discrete, repetitive tasks that could be performed by essentially unskilled workers. The concept was especially suited to the use of untrained immigrants, who then were flooding into the U.S., in mass production industries. (In 1910, 31.9 percent of all people engaged in manufacturing and mechanical jobs were foreign born.) Jobs were redesigned, reduced to their simplest biomechanical elements, largely to escape the expense of training the immigrants for more complex jobs. As a result, reported one labor economist, "managers displayed amazing ingenuity in adapting work to unskilled laborers but manifested almost no interest in developing the men themselves."[2]

Because of the economies of scale it made possible, scientific management significantly increased output. It was also remarkably effective in seaprating employees from real involvement in the work process. Taylorism spread widely, especially in the 1920s, and became the reigning organization philosophy of American industry. At the conference, Sam Camens, who saw the results of scientific management when he worked in steel mills in the 1940s and 1950s, vividly describes how it worked.

> . . . you were told when to do something, how to do something, how far you could go. Every job was broken down to its smallest integral part so that, as we said in the plants, 'You could hire any dumb honky off the boat and put him into the plant, and he could do the job.' . . . And it developed a perception in America that you've got to guard a worker, that he can't be trusted, that you've got to have a foreman on his back, that he's irresponsible.

Among many implications of American industry's acceptance of this form of work organization, "the industrial system lost its ability to regenerate workers with skills and decision-making capacity," as Rubinstein says.

One of the main goals of participation, then, could be stated as reuniting the worker and the work process. This is easily stated but difficult to accomplish. The manager who was brought up in this system, and is limited by it, tends to use discipline and other methods of control to pull together fragmented production processes, and the tendency of the worker is to resist. When a union is present, the primary struggle is reflected at another level, between the worker's representative and the manager as they negotiate the terms and conditions of work. Therefore, cooperative efforts can be carried on at the two different levels, on the plant floor where the work is done, and between union and management officials.

In the first several decades of mass production, the spread of scientific management techniques drove the two sides further apart. Workers resisted the fragmentation of jobs and the growing, arbitrary power of foremen through wildcat strikes and the practice of "soldiering," or restraining output. In the end, however, they could not prevent employers, who were buttressed legally by the right of private property and economically by a great pool of unskilled immigrants, from organizing work as they saw fit. Mass production and job specialization had proved so fruitful for employers in terms of productivity improvement, that the division and subdivision of skills accelerated. Instead of increasing the worker's involvement in the work process, basic industry was moving in the opposite direction.

Very early in this industrializing process there seems to have been some naysayers who urged a return to the cooperation that once existed between masters and journeymen. A few experiments involving the formation of "shop councils" of workers and managers to solve production problems were even recorded in the early 1900s.[3] But what we now call worker participation—reforms on the shop floor—was not the object of the first large-scale cooperative projects between organized labor and management. Among the first was formation of the National Civic Federation, organized by Samuel Gompers, president of the American Federation of Labor, and prominent industrialists such as Senator Marcus Hanna. By providing mediation and conciliation services, the Federation had the laudable goal of reducing labor strife. But the involvement of top-level union leaders tended to blunt their militancy at a time when many corporations were intent on destroying trade unions. "Labor-management cooperation" of this form earned a bad name, probably deservedly. Long before 1920, the Civic Federation lost whatever stature it once had with labor, and it was finally abolished in 1935.

During World War I, unions grew rapidly under the protection of the federal government. The National War Labor Board, consisting of labor, management, and neutral members, encouraged collective bargaining and the spread of unionism as a means of ensuring labor peace. Adopting a concept already tried with success in wartime England, the Board ordered shop committees installed in many plants, thereby moving the cooperative process to the shop-floor level on a widespread basis. The committees discussed workers' grievances, wages, hours, and working conditions. In only a relatively few cases, however, did the committees engage in problem-solving, of the kind that dominates today's team activities, to improve productivity and quality.[4]

One unintended effect (unintended, at least, by the unions) of this cooperative endeavor was the postwar spread of company unions. Gompers and other labor members of the board did not object to the formation of shop committees in 125 companies, many of them non-union. The union leaders expected that the non-union committees would become independent unions. When the Board went out of existence in August, 1918, however, the labor leaders found themselves without power to insist that the committees be absorbed by existing unions. Instead, many of them continued as company unions, dominated by management. As such, they helped management defeat union organizing attempts.[5]

The movement started by the wartime committees expanded rapidly after the war and merged with two other trends that dealt serious blows to unionism. One was an overtly anti-union drive known as the American Plan. This was a well-organized, national effort by corporations, trade groups such as the National Association of Manufacturers, and conservative political groups to replace union shops and closed shops with the open shop concept. Clothed in rhetoric that painted unions as unAmerican and unnecessary, American Plan sponsors succeeded in eliminating organized labor from many sectors of the economy.

The second major trend of the 1920s, known as Welfare Capitalism, arose out of a somewhat more benign and paternalistic spirit, though it often occurred hand-in-hand with the American Plan. By the 1920s, some "enlightened" employers had come to the conclusion that "the labor problem" had not been, and could not be, solved by treating workers like any other commodity used in production. Moreover, there was a sense in the early 1920s, following the reelection of President Calvin Coolidge, that "American capitalism was triumphant not only politically and materially but also spiritually."[6]

Then employers began changing their employment policies to treat workers in a more humane way. A new managerial function, personnel management, was added to the growing technocratic structure on industry to administer the new policy in a "scientific" way. The personnel managers took over hire-and-fire decisions from foremen and designed relatively comprehensive industrial relations policies. Workers were promised a "fair wage," reasonable working hours, and hygenic working conditions. Life and disability insurance, old-age pensions, profit-sharing, and stock purchase plans were offered to workers. Shop committees were installed as an integral part of the new policy.

As a result of these converging trends, the number of shop committees shot up from 225 in 1919 to 814 in 1924.[7] They were the fad of the day in American industry. The committees allowed workers some voice in the workplace—although of course, management had the last word—and so passed (for a time) as an alternative to collective bargaining. The Wagner Act of 1935 outlawed company unions. But organized labor has a very long memory, and many union leaders remain convinced that non-union employers today also use shop-floor committees (under the faddish name of quality circles) largely to foil organizing attempts.

The 1920s also saw a number of cooperative experiments in workplaces where bonafide, independent unions represented employees. In retrospect, however, these episodes did little to enhance the reputation of cooperation, largely because they occurred alongside the anti-union efforts under the American Plan and Welfare Capitalism. Indeed, they are frequently cited as examples of how unions can delude themselves. This negative perspective grew out of the labor climate of the 1920s.

It was a bad decade for organized labor. Under seige by combative employers and unable to organize the growing mass production industries, some unions in highly competitive industries reversed their once-militant opposition to any cooperation that smacked of "class collaboration." In 1923, Gompers called industry and labor to "legislate in peace, to find the way forward in collaboration." He urged unions to help employers become more efficient in order to demonstrate that labor was not only interested in winning "more." Labor, he said, "is not asking for a chance to get. Labor is asking for a chance to *give*."[8]

Cooperative efforts sprang up in several industries, especially apparel and transportation. Perhaps the best-known, and one of the longest-lived, was at the Baltimore & Ohio Railroad. In 1923, the B & O and the International Association of Machinists began setting up local worker-supervisor committees in repair shops and eventually extended them throughout the system. These committees discussed a wide range of subjects, including efficient utilization of equipment, improvement of operating and maintenance services, and better conditions in the shops. The experiment proved successful in many ways: employee grievances plummeted, union workers were given work that formerly had been contracted out to non-union shops, and senior employees were guaranteed continued employment when business fell (although junior workers were laid off), and the railroad increased its earnings relative to competitors.

It is unclear, from many descriptions of the B & O Plan, the degree to which rank-and-file workers actively participated in committee meetings. Some obviously did, but the lack of data makes it difficult to compare these committees with today's QWL groups and LMPTs. An analysis of suggestions made either directly by workers or through their representatives shows that many of the same types of issues were discussed then as today. As might be expected, given the generally poor working conditions of the 1920s, 20 percent of all worker suggestions pertained to what are today called "comfort" items: cleaner shops, better washroom facilities, improved ventilation and heating, etc. Of 1,076 worker suggestions at the B & O, 7.7 percent related to labor-saving devices or methods, 12 percent to the use of new machinery to eliminate heavy work, and 29.3 percent to shortages of materials and tools. These percentages, says one labor historian, lead "inescapably to the conclusion that union-management cooperation had helped to increase output."[9]

The B & O Plan also faced many of the same impediments as today's participation efforts: the resistance of foremen, attacks by leftist union groups, union factionalism, delays by management in carrying out suggested changes, disinterest of top-level managers at some shops, and growing worker disgruntlement over the lack of some means to measure and share the gains. Nevertheless, the plan exhibited a remarkable sustaining power. The committees kept meeting until 1941, although suggestions relating to labor-saving devices, not surprisingly, dropped off drastically with the onset of the Depression.

The 1920s saw four other important examples of union-management cooperation, though none emphasized the shop-committee approach. In Cleveland, garment manufacturers and the International Ladies' Garment Workers Union stabilized employment by determining production methods and time study on a joint basis. The Amalgamated Clothing Workers helped preserve the men's apparel industry by negotiating wage cuts in return for a voice in production standards and other matters. Similar programs occurred in the Philadelphia hosiery industry and at the New England textile company. The common element in these cases, as well as on the railroads, was growing competition from non-union competitors.[10]

Judging the success or failure of the experiments of the 1920s depends largely on one's point of view. Sumner H. Slichter, a labor economist and advocate of participation, concluded of the B & O Plan that it clearly improved morale and relations between "the men and their unions on the one hand and the management on the other."[11] From the vantage point of the 1980s, that may not seem like much, especially if viewed by unions who seek concrete gains through gainsharing and increased union voice in operation of the company. Furthermore, the union-management cooperation of the 1920s retains a bad odor for many observers because of the climate in which it originated. "All in all," concluded the noted labor historians Selig Perlman and Philip Taft, "union-management cooperation was the program of a spiritually defeated unionism."[12]

It is historically inaccurate, however, to include these few examples of union-management cooperation in the much larger bag of anti-union efforts in the 1920s and judge the all as defective. In any case, most of the programs died out in the Depression, if not before. Unlike today's worker participation movement, they were confined to a few industries (and a few companies within those industries) and did not develop a body of principles and techniques. The parallels cited by the participation critics of the 1980s are evanescent at best.

Although certain features of the union-management cooperation of 60 years ago were similar to those in play today, the experiences of the two eras are substantially different. Speaking only of cooperative efforts in the union sector, they were confined in the 1920s to the railroad and apparel industries. Today, they can be found in all basic manufacturing industries and exist on a far wider scale.

The next period of labor-management cooperation was World War II, when the federal government, once again, encouraged unionism and collective bargaining to ensure continued production for the war effort. At the prompting of the War Production Board, close to 5,000 joint committees were established in plants employing nearly seven million workers; but these quickly dissolved after the war. According to one study, only 287 committees were still operating in 1948. Moreover, their potential for addressing issues of substance was not realized, largely because employers feared the erosion of their authority on management rights issues.[13]

More than 40 years later, it is painfully apparent that American management discarded a brilliant opportunity in the wartime years. At no time before or since (with the possible exception of the 1980s) was the situation of industry so ripe for establishing labor-management cooperation. Winning the war was only one reason for doing so. Another was the need to construct a new industrial relations system to replace the turmoil and warfare that had existed since the birth of industrial unionism in the late 1930s. The infant unions in basic industry had won the struggle for recognition under the law, and now they were searching for a permanent role in industry and society. Such a role was proposed by Philip Murray, president of the CIO and founder of the United Steelworkers, and Walter Reuther, a young leader of the United Auto Workers who would become its president in 1947.

They and other CIO officials in 1940, and again at the outset of the war in 1941, urged the government to create "industry councils" in each basic defense industry. With a membership of top-level union and management leaders, each council would coordinate production decisions for an entire industry. This partnership would extend into the plants, where shop-floor committees would collaborate in solving production problems.

The shop-floor aspect of this idea grew partly out of the experiences of the USW during its formative years in the late 1930s. Its predecessor organization, the Steel Workers Organizing Committee (SWOC), invited companies to participate in joint union-management efforts to raise productivity. This effort, led by a Murray lieutenant named Clinton S. Golden, was successful in several smaller companies and even succeeded in saving a few firms from bankruptcy. A local union leader at one of these companies was Joseph Scanlon, who joined SWOC's staff and later devised a scheme for combining the worker participation in problem-solving with a formula which enabled labor to share in the monetary gains realized by increased productivity. Known as the Scanlon Plan, this approach is now used by several hundred American companies.

Under Golden's influence, Murray also agreed to co-author a 1940 book which advocated that management "invite labor's cooperation in the management processes." Murray and his co-author, Morris L. Cooke, an industrial engineer and disciple of Frederick Taylor, based their concept on a psychology of the worker that organization development specialists began to talk about 20 years later. "The goal of all industrial organizations must be to make it possible for every worker to give the best that he has in him. That is the meaning of individuality; the foundation of self-respect and pride."[14]

Reuther also believed that workers should contribute ideas, as well as brawn, in the workplace. He, himself, created a public stir in 1941 by proposing that the auto industry retool some of its plants to mass produce planes for the war effort.

Despite evidence that the plan might have worked, industry leaders rejected it, suggesting in their statements that only management had the right to think up bold ideas. Management also believed that the CIO unions, by proposing industry councils, were bent on seizing control of industry. It was no surprise, then, that the War Production Board ignored Murray's proposal and, instead, urged companies and unions to establish plant-level, labor-management committees. Many of these committees aided the war effort, largely by keeping worker morale at a high pitch, but they did not result in labor gaining decision-making powers. Management, by and large, was not ready to listen to what workers had to say. "There will be none of this equal voice bunk at GM," Charles Wilson, president of General Motors, said.[15]

Management's attitude demonstrated a failure of understanding that would have dreadfully ironic consequences three decades later. At the end of the war, the unions put aside ideas of establishing a partnership with management and adopted a reactive bargaining role, one focused on controlling the fragmented job system already in place. Murray and the Steelworkers forgot about their pioneering participation efforts and concentrated on raising wages. In collective bargaining, the unions tied their wage demands to specific jobs, not workers, put work-rule barriers around those jobs, and denied any responsibility for making the work process efficient. It was management's responsibility to manage the business, they said. In the 1970s, the growth of foreign competition made this role increasingly obsolete, and management began suggesting a more participative relationship. By this time, however, job-control unionism was embedded solidly in societal concrete.

Although the World War II committees did not last long, they did lay the foundations for a forward-looking program sponsored by the Federal Mediation and Concilliation Service. In the 1970s, the FMCS helped establish two dozen regional and citywide labor-management committees, which have fostered cooperative programs in their areas. For the most part, however, the experiments with shop committees in the 1920s and 1940s

did not spread and become a permanent part of the labor relations system; indeed, they left a legacy of suspicion regarding
their origins and effectiveness. Nevertheless, there remained
alive a persistent undercurrent of feeling, buttressed by increasing awareness of the authoritarian nature of industrial discipline
and the grave health and safety problems in mines and factories,
that significant reforms were needed.

In the 1930s, Elton Mayo and his colleagues at Harvard
University carried out their famous, though inconclusive, stud-
ies at Western Electric's Hawthorne plant in Cicero, Ill. Convinced that work should be a cooperative endeavor, Mayo advocated the use of autonomous work groups (though this term was
not used until much later). Employers ignored his advice, largely
because, Mayo caustically concluded, most managers still sub-
scribed to the "rabble hypothesis"—that mankind is a horde of
unorganized individuals actuated by self-interest (financial incentive is the only effective human motive) and incapable of sustained cooperation. In other words, the teachings of scientific
management still held sway.[16]

In the 1950s and 1960s, specialists in organizational behavior and industrial psychology began to develop a body of theory
to support the reorganization of work along the path suggested
by Mayo. In Britain, Eric Trist and his associates at the Tavistock
Institute of Human Relations began experiments as early as
1949 with autonomous work teams in the coal industry. This was
the origin of the socio-technical systems (STS) concept, which
holds that the social and technical organization of work must be
integrated; the individual worker must be treated as comple-
mentary to the machine rather than as an extension of it. Refine-
ments and modifications of STS were studied by various experts
in Australia, Norway, and the United States, including Einar
Thorsrud of Norway, Fred Emery of Australia, and Louis E.
Davis of America.[17]

At about the same time, forward-looking management in
the United States began to listen to a new generation of industrial psychologists and organizational development specialists,
including Abraham Maslowe, Douglas McGregor, Frederick
Hertzberg, Rensis Likert, and Chris Argyris. Their ideas for reform were provocative but perhaps a bit too advanced for the

1960s, when they began to be heard. Instead of initiating full-scale reforms, management translated these concepts into a partial redesign of jobs by adding duties to narrow occupations and giving certain employees more discretion in performing their jobs. Out of this short-lived trend came the terms "job enlargement," "job enrichment," and "matrix management." Companies tended to apply these reforms only to managerial jobs; blue-collar workers were seldom involved.

Nevertheless, this was an important development in the growing trend toward real worker participation. Along with the autonomous work group experiments in Britain, Norway, and Sweden, the redesign efforts in the United States began to produce an invaluable body of theory and empirical data. Gradually, the concept that work not only should be, but could be, reformed seeped into the industrial consciousness, if not yet that of the nation.

The 1960s also brought more evidence that something was wrong in industrial America. The coming of industrial unions in the 1930s, of course, had done much to alleviate poor working conditions. Through collective bargaining and sophisticated grievance procedures, unions gave voices to millions of ordinary workers in a representative industrial democracy. This was a large step forward, but it fell short of the longer shadow cast by rising expectations about work and its rewards in the aftermath of World War II. Of necessity, unions devoted their energies and resources to battling for wage raises and new or improved benefits, such as pensions, medical insurance, layoff pay, and more paid time off the job.

By the early 1960s, it was becoming apparent that these monetary rewards, although still of prime importance, did not satisfy fully increasing numbers of union members. A wave of vague discontent and alienation swept through heavy industry, particularly the giant, impersonal plants of the auto and steel industries. Many factors were involved. The introduction of new production technologies spurred an automation scare and the fear of a wholesale loss of jobs. The civil rights revolution entered the factories, leading to demands for better jobs by blacks and demands for seniority protection by whites. Safety and health had become matters of greater concern. Awakened by television's focus on the comfortable lifestyle of white-collar workers, blue-collar workers also began to demand amenities accorded to salaried workers—better parking lots, cleaner workplaces, protection from layoffs, and more control over their jobs. (Walter Reuther even proposed, in 1961, that hourly workers be placed on salary, a demand that management dismissed out-of-hand.)

Meanwhile, recessions of the late 1950s and early 1960s, combined with government pressure for price restraint and the beginnings of import competition, had forced management to seek greater efficiencies in the workplace. To do this, the companies typically used old style management methods of discipline and control. They made unilateral changes in work practices, slowed down the grievance-handling process, and put pressure on foremen to get tougher with the workers. This was no longer the contented 1950s, management said; it was time to hold the union at the bridge. Predictably, the workers chafed at the increasing authoritarianism.

Their response was partly a revolt against dictatorial bosses and partly a revolt against union leaders' control of collective bargaining at the company-wide or industry-wide level. Now, the local unions demanded autonomy in negotiating issues involving working conditions in the plants. This trend was most dramatically manifested in the auto industry. The United Auto Workers had fared better than most unions in democratizing the workplace and raising the living standards of its members. Nevertheless, in the bargaining years of 1961 and 1964, the UAW suddenly was confronted by what might be characterized as a large-scale rebellion in the ranks. In the past, Reuther and his lieutenants had negotiated economic issues on a company-wide basis and allowed the UAW locals to discuss local matters with plant management. But the local talks were considered secondary and were to be concluded by the time Reuther reached agreement at the national level. In 1961 and 1964, scores of UAW locals ignored the rules and went on strike over local issues, even after a national settlement had been announced. This was particularly true at General Motors Corp.; GM's automotive operations remained shut down for nearly two months by the local strikes in 1964.

It was obvious that the UAW had not devoted enough atten-tion to conditions in the plants. As late as 1964, for example, many GM plants provided only open toilet stalls in washrooms so that supervisors could intimidate workers (the 1964 local work stoppages at GM are still known as the "toilet stall strikes"). The UAW's bargaining procedure also was at fault. It did not give the locals enough time to deal with shop-floor issues nor strike leverage to get them settled. After the 1964 round of strikes, the UAW substantially changed its bargaining procedure to give the locals more power in negotiating local issues.

To what extent did these strikes reveal worker discontent about conditions in the plants? A definitive answer cannot be made, because other factors were involved. To some extent, the strikes grew out of internal political maneuvering in the UAW. Local officers, who had long played a subordinate role to Reu-ther and his powerful, centralized administration, seized the moment to assert themselves and gain increased leverage in local talks. Some local leaders also adopted a militant posture to win reelection. It would be impossible, therefore, to boil off the po-litical element of local-issues bargaining to produce a distilled es-sence of worker dissatisfaction. Attributing the rebelliousness to a growing, if nebulous, discontent over working conditions and management style must remain a matter of subjective judgment. But the demand for local autonomy in bargaining could well have reflected a parallel, if unstated, demand for individual au-tonomy over the job. From the vantage point of the 1980s, how-ever, this conclusion seems valid and has been endorsed by a top-level UAW official.[18]

Local bargaining also became a crucial issue in the steel in-dustry in the 1965 election battle between USW President David J. McDonald and challenger I.W. Abel, the union's secretary-treasurer. The USW had never had a carefully defined proce-dure for its locals to engage in local-issues negotiations with plant managers. Instead, the local unions could only raise plant-level problems in company-wide discussions involving all locals in each company. To obtain satisfaction on his issues, a local union officer had to win the support of USW district directors, International staff members, and, frequently, the union presi-dent. Relatively few local issues managed to find their way through that political maze. When McDonald (who had been president since 1952) finally settled with top-level company negotiators on an industry-wide wage and benefit agreement, the union typically dropped—"washed out" was the term derisively used by dissident local leaders—all unsettled local issues, sometimes totaling several hundred.

The USW's strategy of negotiating with an industry-wide bargaining committee representing up to a dozen steel companies had produced good wage gains. But, it also had the effect of widening the distance between USW leaders and daily problems in the plants. Although Abel's presidential challenge resulted primarily from a revolt against McDonald by a majority of executive board members, the local bargaining issue played an important role. Promising to "return the union to the rank and file," Abel defeated McDonald in one of the first successful overthrows of an entrenched union president in modern labor history. In 1968, Abel instituted a procedure allowing local unions to negotiate plant-level agreements, and in 1973, they also gained the right to strike over local issues.[19]

Neither the steel nor the auto example proves a linear cause-effect relationship between poor working conditions and the so-called, blue-collar blues. It is impossible to precisely quantify expectations, aspirations and attitudes and relate them to specific physical events, especially at a time of great social turmoil. But the massive shift to local autonomy in bargaining cannot be adequately explained by citing "union politics." At the very least, it indicated that worker alienation was simmering and bubbling in the 1960s.

This trend, which has gone unnoticed by most historians of worker participation, was a far more important formative force for worker participation than a single event that gained worldwide publicity in 1972. The strike at GM's Lordstown (Ohio) plant was billed as a revolt by young workers against dull, repetitive assembly line work. It may have been partly that; certainly, the Lordstown work force was predominantly young, since the plant had opened only a few years previously. The strike, however, was primarily against a "speedup" on the assembly line, a common management practice that had caused innumerable strikes by old and young workers, in many plants, over many decades. What created headlines for the "Lordstown syndrome" was a certain readiness on the part of society in the early 1970s to be angry about the conditions of work, just as it was angry about air pollution, the Vietnam War, and Watergate. The intellectual elite had taken up the cause, partly because the radical left had rediscovered work issues and partly because the federal government was alarmed about a national slowdown in productivity growth. In addition, the UAW's Lordstown local president was an articulate and effective spokesman for the proposition that assembly line work dehumanized the individual.

The false headlines about the Lordstown syndrome was symptomatic of the times. For almost ten years, starting in the late 1960s, the entire field of work psychology, organizational change, and job reforms was characterized by intellectual confusion, both in the popular press, and in industry. Did the blue-collar blues exist, or were they the figment of an elite imagination? Were the workers of the "baby boom" generation, then entering the workplace in massive numbers, devoid of the *work ethic*—that curious and somewhat mythical quality that each generation believes is lacking in the succeeding generation—or did they require different motivations, different challenges, than their parents? Was the stagnating productivity growth of the period mainly attributable to slackening work effort and multiplying health and safety regulations, as many companies charged, or were innovation and growth being stifled by the hierarchical structure of work and the management bureaucracies spawned by it? The debate went on, but to observers on the outside, nothing seemed to come of it.

This perception was not entirely wrong, for the great majority of companies—especially in manufacturing—continued to blame their increasing competitive problems on rising labor costs, decreasing effort, and growing government regulation. On the union side, a smug contentedness in upper echelons (with only a few exceptions) swept aside all suggestions that the democratization of the workplace—once a crusading mission for the unions created by the Congress of Industrial Organizations (CIO))—had not advanced much beyond primitive levels.

In retrospect, it can be seen that all the sound and fury of those years both stimulated and obscured work reform efforts that were to be the generating phase for what burst forth in the 1980s. In addition to the well-known work enrichment and enlargement disciples, a few consultants and managers patiently were developing deeper concepts of reform, trying them out in practice, and learning from their mistakes. Most of this happened in non-union firms. The most publicized example was General Foods' Pet Foods plant in Topeka, where workers were organized into self-managed teams. Started in the early 1970s, the Topeka project was successful for awhile, suffered from the unfriendly attitude of corporate executives and the loss of key personnel, but managed to survive into the 1980s.

Sid Rubinstein had begun working with unions and companies in a variety of industries as far back as 1959. His special contribution was integrating quality control systems with social systems (for example, the structure of management, the organization of work, and union-management relations). Elsewhere in this book, Rubinstein's candid description of how his concepts changed and evolved over a 20-year period, largely through trial and error, is an invaluable addition to the literature of worker participation.

Meanwhile, the intellectuals of worker participation continued to produce papers and hold conferences. Although their theories and abstract constructions of the ideal workplace seemed remote from working America, the intellectuals in the end began to pull industrialists and a few unionists into their orbit. It was at a conference of such experts at Harriman, N.Y. in 1972 that Louis Davis of the University of California introduced the term "quality of working life" (QWL) as a generic label for a wide variety of work innovations that emphasize individual autonomy.

The first large breakthrough in the unionized sector was a joint QWL program negotiated by the UAW and GM in 1973. Over the next several years, GM and the UAW initiated a number of work reforms at various plants, but it was a slow process. Irving Bluestone, then a UAW vice president and the chief negotiator at GM, had to pull a reluctant union along with him. GM management, in many plants, also resisted deep-seated changes in the work process, preferring to limit gains to an improved labor relations climate.

For several years, experiments in GM plants were kept secret: not until 1979 did the two sides talk publicly about their most successful program, at GM's Tarrytown (New York) plant. Even there, the results were mixed. Rubinstein's account of QWL's incomplete development at Tarrytown, told here for the first time, shows how caution and lack of experience prevented the UAW and GM from achieving fundamental reforms.

But the Tarrytown experiment was a beginning, and there were many other beginnings in the mid-to-late 1970s. Among the most notable were programs at Sidney Harmon's automotive mirror plant in Bolivar, Tenn. (with the UAW) and at GM's Packard-Electric Division in Warren, Ohio (with the International Union of Electrical Workers). By 1979, it was apparent that large sections of America's manufacturing sector were mired in deep, competitive trouble. Imports from many nations, but especially Japan, were flooding the American market. Struggling with high overhead and labor costs, large and unproductive management bureaucracies, and the public's (correct) perception of poor product quality, the producers of autos, steel, electronic products, tires, construction machinery, and many other basic goods rapidly lost market share.

It was about this time that many employers, seeking a quick fix and looking to Japan for guidance, began to adopt the quality circle concept. Something was working right in Japan, so the thinking went, and it seemed to involve management's ability to gain labor's cooperation on the shop floor. The most visible evidence of this in Japanese companies was the quality control circle, a committee of workers and foremen that met weekly to discuss and solve production problems relating to quality.

Furthermore, many Japanese industries appear to have invested line managers with responsibility for establishing shop-floor teamwork, instead of shunting it to a staff specialist in labor relations or organizational development. Indeed, quality control circles were not installed as a labor relations program, but rather, as part of an integrated management effort to improve quality. The Japanese, in fact, rejected other American concepts suggested by U.S. advisors in the early 1950s, including detailed job descriptions.[20]

In the late 1970s, 25 years later, some American companies

understood what they were copying as they installed quality circles. But many others thought of the quality circle as an employee relations mechanism, an expanded form of the old suggestion box system: the company gives workers a few hours' training in analytical techniques, provides a room and a table, and tells them to think up suggestions. One efficacious thing about this process is that discussion among many people is more likely to produce good ideas than a single worker's monologue to the audience of a suggestion box. But if participation is limited to this procedure, it is a restricted form both of employee involvement and integrated quality control. The workers have little voice at the second and third levels of Rubinstein's three-tier structure, and virtually no possibility of exerting an influence on strategic business decisions. Moreover, fundamental work restructuring occurs only by management fiat.

Quality circles spread rapidly in American industry from 1979 on. One survey found that 713 companies had installed 12,424 quality circles in 1,572 locations by 1982.[21] A more recent estimate is that more than 90% of the *Fortune* "500" companies have quality circle programs.[22] A large number of quality circles die within a few years, particularly those that are adopted merely to collect workers' ideas and not as a step toward a new management style. This type of program can be invigorating for companies and workers for a short period of time, but one danger is that workers inevitably begin to feel that they are being manipulated to produce cost savings without a compensating change in their wages or work lives. On the other hand, managers can use quality circles as "an interim or transitional device in moving toward a more participative management system and culture." But this has happened only rarely.[23]

Since the early 1980s, cooperative efforts of all kinds have multiplied rapidly. The major stimulus has been economic adversity: two recessions from 1980 to 1983, a rising flood of imports caused by the strength of the dollar versus other currencies and the concurrent growth of low-wage competition in Third World countries, and deregulation of the trucking, airline, and telephone industries. It became obvious that the bankruptcies and massive job losses during this period were not the result of a simple downward swing of the business cycle, which would be followed—as always in the postwar era—by an upward swing.

Aware that fundamental changes were under way, labor and management in hundreds of plants and offices decided to put aside old animosities and try "a new way." Bargaining over wages and benefits remained an adversary procedure, but a mutual desire for survival motivated employers and unions to form various kinds of shop-floor committees, teams and task groups devoted to cutting costs, reducing waste and making the production process more efficient. As a *quid pro quo* for wage concessions, some unions won other infringements on management control, such as seats on boards of directors (at Chrysler, Pan Am, Eastern Air Lines, and nearly a dozen smaller companies), a voice in hiring and layoff policies (General Motors, Ford), and substantial stock ownership in many firms. Some observers use the term "concession bargaining" to imply that workers give up far more than they gain in these deals. A term that more accurately describes what happens in these bargains was coined by Randy Barber, director of the Center for Economic Organizing and a union consultant who advised the Eastern unions. He uses "reciprocal bargaining" to refer to an agreement in which workers, management, stockholders, creditors, customers, and suppliers all make reciprocal sacrifices for the good of the organization.

Unquestionably, the fear of people whose jobs and careers were at risk was the immediate spur for large numbers, probably the majority, of these efforts. But another underlying and very powerful current soon became apparent. By the 1980s, the baby boom generation dominated the American workplace in terms of numbers. These workers brought with them a much higher level of education than previous generations, as well as social values that had been formed during the civil rights and anti-establishment turmoil of the 1960s. They wanted more challenging, interesting work and a greater measure of control over their jobs and workplace environment. Problem-solving committees, autonomous work teams and other varieties of participation offer an involvement that appeals to a growing number of rank-and-file workers. Their enthusiasm for the process is quickly noted by anyone who talks to employees in the workplace and at meetings such as the 1984 Leadership Conference.

Perhaps fear drove people to participation, but once that Pandora's Box opened wide, revealing the possibilities of personal fulfillment and the institutional strengths of cooperation, a new element was added. People like the feeling of control and will continue to support the revolution (and the participation movement *is* working a revolution, albeit a gradually unfolding one, in work practices and relations) as long as it meets their needs. In some plants where I have observed cooperative efforts, workers declare outright that they will not give up their new forms of participation without a struggle.

Although the participation movement has begun to effect permanent change, it still faces many challenges. Among other things, it now must move from a plateau of simple problem-solving to higher peaks of employee involvement. Some companies and unions are already on the march. But many questions must be answered, including the following:

1. Can unions discard their old job classification systems and permit management to operate under more flexible rules with regard to work assignment? One of the lingering vestiges of scientific management is the present structure of job classification in most industries. When the industrial unions came on the scene of the 1930s and 1940s, they found work already divided into narrow unskilled and semi-skilled specialties. Focusing then on raising their members' standard of living, the unions accepted this organization of work and codified it in their labor agreements.

Now that management has discovered the competitive need to move to more flexible arrangements (wider job classifications, rotating work assignments, and autonomous work teams based on a "pay-for-knowledge" compensation system), many unions are balking. Changes are occurring in relatively few work locations, including the exciting GM-Toyota joint venture in Fremont, California, and it is planned for GM's Saturn plant in Tennessee. The latter, which will combine new technology and a highly participative work system, was planned by a committee of managers and workers. It is important to note that this major example of using the socio-technical approach to plant design and operation did not suddenly pop up as a "good idea." It was the culmination of 12 years of joint experimentation with participation concepts between the UAW and GM.

There are other examples of a gradual restructuring of work and job classifications. In some steel, auto, and rubber plants, unions allow machine operators to perform minor maintenance work. By-and-large, however, local unions are resisting widespread reform in this area, even though combining and enlarging duties—if it is accomplished without favoritism—is desired by many workers. This change is of such magnitude that, in the end, it may only be achieved as part of a mature participation process.

2. Can companies overcome their traditional reliance on layoffs to balance demand and production? The lack of job security is one of the biggest impediments in the way of gaining worker commitment to change. But laying off when the business gets into trouble is so deeply rooted in American practice, that many managements refuse to consider alternatives such as those proposed by Rubinstein. He estimates that up to 10% of surplus manpower can be kept on the job for as much as two years. Excess employees, for example, could be kept on the payroll while undergoing training in new skills and problem-solving techniques, or they could replace workers assigned full-time to finding solutions to quality problems and production bottlenecks. (Rubinstein's introductory chapter describes such a plan in one steel plant).

In the same context, it must be asked whether management can also overcome its aversion to sharing business plans with workers. Union officials understandably feel betrayed when, after leading their members into a participative process on the basis of trusting the company, they are suddenly confronted with a major management decision to layoff people or shift production to another plant. In such a situation, worker participation obviously has come to a halt somewhere below the level where important strategic business decisions are made. This does not suggest that participation inevitably must lead to a flooding of boards of directors with workers, although board representation should not be arbitrarily ruled out.

Actually, union officials have won equal or greater access to decision-making in some auto plants than board membership would afford. Being a minority of one on a corporate board confers more status than voting power. On the other hand, some local UAW leaders have a voice in all important work force decisions—including layoffs, transfers, the introduction of technology, and even bidding for new work—in some Ford and GM plants. This process occurs on an informal basis, typically only where labor-management relations have been improved significantly by a participation program and, most important, where the plant manager does not feel threatened by sharing power. Conversely, it happens only where union officials are willing to accept partial responsibility for business decisions—a concept that goes against the grain of American unionism's reactive role.

3. Can unions and companies find a way to use the participation process to introduce changes in collective bargaining agreements? Until now, most labor agreements have specified that problem-solving teams must not deal with any questions that would require contractual modifications. The reason, of course, is the unions (and frequently companies) do not want to make the "important" rules of their relationship amenable by ad hoc teams of workers and supervisors. But this requirement creates dual processes for change, one being the negotiating process for modifying wages, benefits and many work rules and conditions (such as job classifications), and the other being the participation process for introducing changes in all other work practices.

This barrier often frustrates problem-solving teams. Although it would be unwise to throw open to change by anyone, at any time, all items in a labor agreement, it is also doubtful that parallel change processes can exist side-by-side in a highly participative relationship. Walter Reuther's theory of the labor agreement as a "living document" may have to be reintroduced and somehow made to fit individual circumstances. In order to do this, the ad hoc groups must be invested with authority and must exercise it responsibly. One of the strengths of the three-tier approach of Participative Systems, Inc. is that worker-supervisor teams can be trusted with that authority.

4. Can U.S. labor law and government policy accommodate the large changes needed if worker participation is to be institutionalized on a national basis? The National Labor Relations Act (NLRA) of 1935 enshrines the principle of adversary labor-management relations. It essentially freezes statutorily the con-

ditions and philosophy that prevailed in the 1930s. Few people on either side of the bargaining table contend that the adversary principle should be eliminated in wage negotiations. But, that principle also affects other aspects of a relationship.

For instance, the law prohibits employers from forming company-dominated unions. This is a wise provision, considering the history of employer attempts to avoid unions by creating pseudo-participation mechanisms which, in reality, manipulated workers. Unfortunately, many non-union companies today install QWL committees, similarly lacking in real participatory features, to fend off union organizing. A number of union suits against this practice are pending at various levels of the National Labor Relations Board procedure. Eventually, the Board will have to face this issue in a major case. Many non-union companies, however, have deep and meaningful participation programs which could be at risk if an eventual board ruling against false participation are construed too broadly.

There is yet another legal disincentive for unions in some cases to aggressively seek more participation in decision-making for its members. In 1983, the U.S. Supreme court ruled that professors at Yeshiva University performed managerial functions inasmuch as they helped decide curriculum and had a voice on faculty appointments. They, therefore, were exempted from coverage under the NLRA and could not be certified as a collective bargaining unit. This presents what Albert Shanker, president of the American Federation of Teachers, calls a "Catch 22 dilemma." For unions of professionals, Shanker warns, "our laws say that the more employees are able to participate in management decisions, the greater is the danger they will lose their ability under law to bargain collectively."[24]

It is most unlikely that Congress, in drafting the original NLRA and its later amendments, intended to discourage greater employee involvement in the workplace. The law, however, could turn out to have that effect, depending on its interpretation. What can be done? Although one hesitates to urge the amendment of a law that has served the country so well for 50 years, a full-scale national commitment to participation would come about more quickly if the law were updated. But the

NLRA, paradoxically, is under the protection of an impregnable political sanctity conferred upon it by the hostility between national labor and business organizations. No mention of amendment can be made by either side without incurring the immediate opposition of the other side, regardless of the issue at stake. This ideological standoff at the national level will probably delay, and perhaps prevent, a full flowering of participation in the factories and offices where it is needed and wanted.

One hopeful sign indicating the government's advocacy of participative programs was the 1982 creation of a new Labor Department unit, now called the Bureau of Labor-Management Relations and Cooperative Programs. Although the Bureau has confined its activities to holding conferences, developing publications, conducting research, and providing information and networking of people and ideas, all of these activities have helped make a more cooperative approach to labor relations an alternative worth exploring. These are useful activities, and the Bureau employs and is led by dedicated people; but, more needs to be done. Up until the 1970s, the Department of Labor played an activist role in developing labor issues. The Department no longer possesses this power, due in large part to extensive changes such as deregulation, decentralized bargaining, and many other factors. But, despite this, perhaps the Bureau is the first indication of yet another reevaluation of the Department's role in developing an alternative to traditional labor-management relations.

Although the federal government can be faulted for a lack of leadership, it cannot be blamed for the institutional barriers to participation that have been thrown up by companies and unions. In some respects, unions may have advanced further down the road to acceptance than management. At least four unions now have important participation clauses embedded in contracts with nationwide corporations. They are the USW (in the steel, aluminum, and container industries), the UAW, the Communications Workers of America (at AT&T), and the International Union of Electrical Workers (at GM). In addition, large numbers of local unions engage in participative programs, even if their national and international leaders remain opposed.

But many union officials still express doubts about management sincerity, and some unionists continue to condemn participation as a betrayal of "working-class interests."

As a whole, organized labor is moving, although glacially, toward adopting participation as a "demand." Only five years ago, for example, AFL-CIO leaders—whose opposition or advocacy on certain issues can set a national tone for labor-management relations—seldom had anything positive to say about participation. By February 1985, the situation had changed drastically. The AFL-CIO Committee on the Evolution of Work pointed out, in a major report, that surveys had disclosed "a particular insistence voiced by workers, union and non-union alike, to have a say in the 'how, why, and wherefore' of their work" which could be met by union-management programs affording worker participation in decision-making. "The labor movement should seek to accelerate this development," the report declared, although cautioning that "some employers have used quality of work life programs as 'union avoidance measures' or as simple 'speed-up' efforts."[25]

This statement may not seem to exude passion for the participation concept (after all, it is a diluted extract of a committee's pondering), but it represents a significant change in position. Perhaps even more telling are recent comments by Thomas R. Donahue, the AFL-CIO secretary-treasurer, chairman of the Committee on the Evolution of Work, and the federation's chief spokesman on participation for several years. Unions and employers will continue to bargain, and sometimes fight, over the distribution of profits, Donahue said, adding: "But . . . that confrontation between union and employer ought to be limited to that period of negotiation and should be replaced for the much longer period of contract life by a spirit of cooperation.[26]

Most union leaders still hold a passive position on participation when compared to statements made by Lynn Williams of the Steelworkers. It is important to repeat and emphasize his comments on participation at the Leadership Conference:

> I don't believe this movement will live and succeed in America except in places where there is trade union representation. That's why I'm not afraid of it. A lot of trade unionists

seem to be frightened of it; frightened of it as an antiunion tool, frightened of it as a way of defeating the labor movement. . . . I'm inclined much more to see it as a way in which to build the labor movement, because I think any company that starts on a participative process and starts honestly and conscientiously with a non-union group, that group . . . will inevitably move in the direction of organization and some kind of collective coming together.

Labor's worst fears about participation have come true in some cases. In a few instances, unions have been decertified by a vote of members after the introduction of a participation program. At the same time, data on organizing success gathered by the AFL-CIO shows that it is difficult, if not impossible, to organize workers who are involved in a QWL program. This may mean that unions will have to offer, in addition to better wages, a more meaningful participation process.

The split-up of AT&T by court order presents a different problem. Although a QWL provision expressing the spirit of participation was accepted on a national basis by AT&T before its division into seven separate companies, it is questionable whether management and union representatives in all of the Bell companies accepted the full implications of the provision. QWL is now thriving in some places, but not in others. In the auto industry, local UAW leaders charged in 1984 that some GM plant managers unilaterally installed QWL programs as management vehicles for increasing productivity. Although there was evidence that the local leaders, themselves, might have erred by refusing to become involved, their complaints led to modifications in the 1984 GM-UAW contract. This might not have been necessary had GM corporate headquarters and the international union closely monitored what was happening at individual plants.

These examples illustrate one issue that most unions and large corporations have yet to solve: how to create a forum at the corporate and international union level for dealing with major changes in the economic environment that can have a negative impact on local participation programs.

At the Packard-Electric division of GM, a highly successful

cooperative program foundered for several months after IUE officials charged that management reneged on a pledge to create jobs in return for union cooperation. Despite the success of the joint program between the Clothing & Textile Workers and Johnson & Johnson at Ethicon's Somerville plant, the union and the company may have mishandled another problem. The ACTWU charged that Johnson & Johnson frustrated organizing attempts at a New Mexico plant by involving non-union employees in a participation program; and the union considered, but rejected, calling a halt to the cooperation at Somerville. The company insists that the New Mexico program was not anti-union. Whatever the facts of the case, the implications were not discussed thoroughly by leaders on both sides.

In the steel industry, Labor-Management Participation Teams collapsed at a number of companies because of plant closings and work force contractions in the 1980s. Some might have been saved had there been more collaboration among high-level leaders on both sides. On the one hand, a local union at one plant stopped cooperating in a successful program on grounds—disputed by the company—that US Steel eliminated jobs in violation of the labor contract. At about the same time, in 1983, USW President Lloyd McBride ordered a halt in all attempts to establish new LMPTs at US Steel. He was angered by a corporate decision to import semi-finished steel slabs from Britain for finishing in American plants, a move that would have cost many American jobs. After McBride died in late 1983, his successor, Lynn Williams, reversed McBride's policy of linkage between commercial decisions and participation. The union could disagree with the company on one issue while continuing to cooperate on others, Williams said. By that time, however, much damage had been done that might have been averted by "a forum at the corporate and international level to constantly review issues for continuity of the participation process," Rubinstein says. "Companies and unions ought to be able to disagree on some issues without losing the effectiveness of what they have already established.

There are other such examples. Indeed, tensions always will exist where continued cooperation between two institutions depends on the very human quality known as trust. Trusts can be broken, either purposely or inadvertently, in countless ways, and labor-management relations are particularly vulnerable. Changes in leadership or philosophy on either side can doom a successful project, as can changes in business conditions, government policy, and in the perceptions of workers over time. This suggests that worker participation, itself, must remain a true, ever-changing process.

At the Leadership Conference, Mike Shay of the ACTWU listed seven objections, involving old principles and perceived rights, that were raised by union members at Ethicon's Somerville plant. As serious as these objections were, Shay concluded," most of us are here because we share the belief that a better alternative to the old pattern of labor-management relations must be found. The old methods no longer work."

Similar questions of principle and rights emerge on management's side of the table. Chief among these is the question of control. It goes against the tradition and ethos of free enterprise in America for management to share control with employees, and many employers will continue to hold to this principle with a grip of *rigor mortis* even as they appear in bankruptcy courts. American management, as a whole, really has never accepted unions as a vital, needed third voice in the economy and society, and any truly participative mechanism must perforce exhibit many of the characteristics of a union. Therefore, one should not anticipate an economy-wide shift to participative management in the near future.

Many employers remain adamantly opposed to unions and fight them vigorously—sometimes using illegal methods—in organizing campaigns. As a consequence, organized labor is withering; by 1985, less than 18 percent of workers in non-agricultural, private companies belonged to unions. The ability of employers to stall unionization using illegal methods and tactics sustains a climate of hostility that continues to force unions and workers to be suspicious of any kind of cooperation, even that which is clearly good for workers.

The corporate opponents of organized labor are likely to be with us for a long time. And so, despite the revolutionary transformations that have occurred in many workplaces, the future for the participation movement can only be described as one of piecemeal gains and reverses, with the gains slowly outpacing the backward steps, in producing fundamental changes in the organization of work and industrial democracy.

REFERENCE NOTES

1. Audrey Freedman, "The New Look in Wage Policy and Employee Relations," New York: The Conference board, Inc., 1985. Eugene Epstein and William C. Freund, *People and Productivity: The New York Stock Exchange Guide to Financial Incentives and the Quality of Work Life,* Homewood, Illinois: Dow Jones-Irwin, 1984. "The 1985 National Survey of Employee Attitudes: Executive Report," New York: Sirota and Alper Associates, Inc., 1985.

    The Sirota and Alper survey results are somewhat surprising in that 23 percent of respondents said they were currently involved in a participation program. In the experience of this writer, and other observers who have visited plants with widely dispersed participation programs, 23 percent seems rather high. The number of workers actively involved in a program at any given time—that is, who regularly attend team meetings, for example—typically does not exceed 10 percent to 15 percent of the work force. The Sirota and Alper question on this issue reads as follows: "A number of organizations have formal employee involvement or participation programs other than employee suggestion programs. These programs are designed to get workers and management together to discuss ways for getting work done better. These programs go by such names as employee involvement teams, quality circles, gainsharing, and so on. Does your organization have such a program?" The possible answers: 1. "Yes, and I have been involved in such a program." 2. "Yes, but I have not been personally involved." 3. "No." 4. "Don't know."

2. Sumner H. Slichter, "The Current Labor Policies of American Industries," *Quarterly Journal of Economics,* May 1929, reprinted in *Potentials of the American Economy: Selected Essays of Sumner H. Slichter,* ed. by John T. Dunlop, Cambridge: Harvard University Press, 1961, p. 184.

3. Henry P. Guzda, "Industrial Democracy: Made in the U.S.A.," *Monthly Labor Review*, May 1984, p. 27.

4. Ron Mitchell, "Rediscovering Our Roots: A History of Quality Circle Activities in the United States from 1918 to 1948," presented at IAQC Annual Conference, Cincinnati, Ohio, April 1984, p. 4.

5. Selig Perlman and Philip Taft, *History of Labor in the United States, 1896–1932*, Volume IV (Labor Movements), New York: The Macmillan Co., 1935.

6. Ibid, p. 580.

7. Mitchell, p. 2.

8. Jean Trepp McKelvey, *AFL Attitudes Toward Production, 1900–1932*, Ithaca, New York: The New York State School of Industrial and Labor Relations, Cornell University, 1952, pp. 84–85.

9. Sumner H. Slichter, *Union Policies and Industrial Management*, Washington: The Brookings Institution, 1941, pp. 445–465.

10. Sanford M. Jacoby, "Union-Management Cooperation in the United States: Lessons from the 1920s," *Industrial and Labor Relations Review*, Volume 37, Number 1, October 1983, p. 27.

11. Slichter (1941), p. 479.

12. Perlman and Taft, p. 584.

13. Dorothea de Schweinitz, *Labor and Management in a Common Enterprise*, Cambridge: Harvard University Press, 1949; cited in *The Operation of Area Labor-Management Committees, Washington, DC: U.S. Department of Labor, 1983, p. 15.*

14. *Morris L. Cooke and Philip Murray, Organized Labor and Production: Next Steps in Industrial Democracy*, New York: Harper and Brothers, 1940; revised edition, 1946, p. 80.

15. Guzda, p. 31.

16. Elton Mayo, *The Social Problems of an Industrial Civilization*, Boston: Harvard University Press, 1945, p. 44.

17. Eric Trist, *The Evolution of Socio-technical Systems: A Conceptual Framework and an Action Research Program*, Ontario: Ontario Quality of Working Life Centre, 1981.

18. Donald Ephlin, UAW Vice President and Director of the General Motors Department, in an interview with the author, 1979.

19. Abel's introduction of plant bargaining did not completely satisfy the steel locals. In 1968 as well as several negotiating years after that, some local unionists charged that Abel, too, washed out their local issues. Unlike the practice of the the McDonald years, however, the local unions in fact met in formal negotiating sessions with plant management and settled many problems.

20. Kenneth Hopper, "Quality, Japan, and the U.S.: The First Chapter," *Quality Progress*, September 1985, pp. 38–40.

21. H. Ned Seelye and Joyce A. Sween, "Quality Circles in the U.S. Industry: Survey Results," *The Quality Circles Journal*, Volume 5.4, November 1982, pp. 26–29. The survey involved 3,175 members of the International Association of Quality Control and, thus, was not based on a representative sample of U.S. industry. Of the companies surveyed, 828 (26.1 percent) responded, and 713 said they had quality circles. Less that 2 percent had installed circles prior to 1979. The number of companies initiating circles in 1979 was 7.1 percent rising to 60.2 percent in 1982.

22. Edward E. Lawler, III and Susan A. Morhman, "Quality Circles after the Fad," *Harvard Business Review*, January-February 1985, p. 66.

23. Ibid, pp. 69–71.

24. News release, Department for Professional Employees, AFL-CIO, October 24, 1985.

25. "The Changing Situation of Workers and Their Unions," a report by the AFL-CIO Committee on the Evolution of Work, February 1985, p. 19.

26. Thomas R. Donahue, "America's Unions—Today and Tomorrow," text of remarks made at the John F. Kennedy School of Government, Harvard University, September 26, 1985.

INDEX